A BADGE, A GUN, BUT NO GOD

The Problems with Policing in America

HILTON NAPOLEON

A BADGE, A GUN, BUT NO GOD
THE PROBLEMS WITH POLICING IN AMERICA

iUniverse books may be ordered through booksellers or by contacting:

iUniverse
1663 Liberty Drive
Bloomington, IN 47403
www.iuniverse.com
844-349-9409

Scripture quotations marked KJV are from the Holy Bible, King James Version (Authorized Version). First published in 1611. Quoted from the KJV Classic Reference Bible, Copyright © 1983 by The Zondervan Corporation.

ISBN: 978-1-6632-3258-8 (sc)
ISBN: 978-1-6632-3257-1 (e)

Library of Congress Control Number: 2021924038

Print information available on the last page.

iUniverse rev. date: 01/13/2022

CONTENTS

09-04-2022

ACKNOWLEDGMENTS

I GIVE THANKS TO GOD the Creator and our Lord and Savior Jesus, who sent favor and healing power from Heaven while I was hospitalized seventy-six days with the Covid 19 virus. This saved my life and allowed me to finish this book.

I give thanks for the wisdom and guidance of my late father, Pastor Harry Nelson Napoleon, leader and shepherd of the Tennessee Missionary Baptist Church for forty-five years. I give thanks to my wonderful mother, Betty Lee Napoleon, who along with my father established my spiritual foundation.

I give thanks for my late brother, Benny Nelson Napoleon, J.D, former Detroit Police Chief and Wayne County Sheriff, who was the guiding influence throughout my law enforcement career. Benny inspired and encouraged me to write this book.

I give special thanks and recognition to my oldest sister, the incomparable, brilliant, world-renowned Dr. Geneva Napoleon Smitherman. She provided me with invaluable guidance and navigated me through the writing process, which allowed me to complete this book.

I would like to recognize my other loving sisters, the late Bobby Napoleon White, Anita Napoleon, Kathryn Napoleon-Brogdon and Sharon Napoleon-Seaton.

Recognition and shout-outs to my children, Alana and Hilton II, step-son, Lamont, and grandchildren, Cierra, Hilton III, Frances, Landon, and all my nieces and nephews.

I extend recognition to my pastor, Bishop Charles H. Ellis III, Senior Pastor, Greater Grace Temple, Detroit, Michigan.

I thank GOD for my "help meet," "my good thing," my wife, Tempie L. Napoleon, whom I love dearly. She exhibited incredible patience and provided impeccable care during my rehabilitation and recuperation from the Covid 19 virus.

This book could not have been completed without Tempie's selflessness and loving care.

1

BLESSED ARE THE PEACEMAKERS

Blessed are the peacemakers, for they shall be called the children of God. (Matthew 5:9)

AS A PEACEMAKER, IT IS a great honor to be called a child of God. Whether you are Baptist, Methodist, Catholic, Protestant, or any other denomination of the Judeo-Christian tradition, this honor comes with tremendous responsibility in serving our citizens. Law enforcement officers must be fully aware of the tremendous ethical responsibilities of their position and must strive to consistently fulfill these responsibilities to the highest professional standards.

Police officers are the official representatives of the government, and they also represent God. No government can exist in a safe, secure environment without police officers responsibly enforcing the laws of the land. Police officers are required to work within the law, and they are entrusted to ensure the rights of all to liberty, equality, and justice.

Being a police officer is one of the most dangerous and stressful jobs in our society. Only those who have worked in that capacity can fully understand what police officers experience on a daily basis. Many brave men and women across this country have given their lives to protect citizens and maintain order.

Being considered a child of God, police officers should take on the nature of God. God represents love, peace, patience, empathy, humility, fairness, courtesy, confidence, righteousness, service, sacrifice, and equality. It is imperative that police departments across the nation make every attempt to recruit candidates who exhibit these attributes.

People who desire to be police officers should love all the people they have sworn to protect and serve. In fact, all of us who serve the public must keep love in the forefront of our minds and hearts. Love is the strongest voice in the world. As police officers, we must utilize the voice of love to unify and strengthen our communities for the greater good. We must utilize love to improve and strengthen our police departments nationwide. Our humanity comes to its fullest bloom when we display a loving disposition. We become a more beautiful society when we give love. As police officers and public servants, this love must not be selective or discriminatory. It must be genuine and true to the public we serve. Can't nothing be love, but love.

Empathy is an important attribute because there are times when police officers come in contact with people of different races, nationalities, and genders. Police officers must be mindful of these differences. They must try to identify with and understand how people of various races and nationalities think and feel. Officers who display sincere empathy will be able to minimize tensions and establish the basis for a calm, stable interaction. Officers without empathy usually escalate situations, making them undesirable. Empathetic officers are extremely valuable assets to police departments nationwide. Their calm demeanor leads to improved community relations and support for their department. When police officers lack empathy towards certain races, it destroys the public trust greatly needed by police departments. An empathic police department is an effective police department.

It is extremely important for departments to have officers who can enforce the laws equally in the communities they serve. In too many cities in America, laws are not enforced equally, causing much strife and anger in black communities. Police departments cannot afford to be one-sided in their enforcement of the law. Police officers must have a strong sense of equality in their treatment of citizens of all races, creed, color, and genders.

People who desire to wear a badge and carry a gun must be willing to sacrifice their safety in order to protect the public from danger. Police officers know the danger of their occupation prior to signing up for the job. They must be willing to sacrifice their well-being when discharging their duties. This is especially true when confronting people suspected of committing crimes. Officers must take the greater risk when investigating suspects. In order to have the proper outcome, this risk includes making absolutely certain that a suspect has a weapon before officers discharge their firearm.

Humility is at the top of the list of attributes that all police officers should have. Displaying a humble demeanor when interacting with citizens is one of the most effective ways to receive cooperation and resolve issues. Displaying humility is not showing weakness. Rather, it actually displays your inner strength. Police officers would be much more revered if they displayed more humility. Police officers who remain humble will be exalted at the proper time.

"Patience is a virtue" is an older expression that should be embodied in every police officer. Officers who exhibit patience produce a calming influence when interacting with the citizens they serve. Patience is the pause that helps officers to get their thoughts back in order and their feelings under control. It gives them the persistence to carry out things that will lead them to long-term success, which will come to those who keep trying.

Courteous police officers go a long way in exhibiting a positive image of their department. It is imperative that police officers are courteous when interacting with blacks and other minorities. Being courteous will ease tensions and provide a better environment for all. When you think of other people as being beneath you, it seeps through your words, behavior, and body language. When you believe that you are better than or superior to others, you may be rude or make assumptions. Remembering that we are all humans, with an innate sense of self-respect, leads to better courtesy in communications.

Considering the present climate and image of police departments nationwide, now is the time to put peace back into the peacemaker. Police officers who are not at peace within themselves will have a difficult time enforcing the laws peacefully. Peace of mind sharpens the five senses, calms down the mind and the emotions, and enables you to focus on mental and physical activities. The more tranquil officers are, the greater is their success, their influence, and their power to do good. Calmness of mind is one of the beautiful jewels of wisdom. Inner peace allows police officers to perform their duties better and allows them to be more positive and productive.

In the law enforcement environment of 2021, there appears to be a severe shortage of God's nature and attributes among police officers, prosecuting attorneys, and police chiefs. Officers are killing unarmed black citizens with alarming regularity, and in many instances, no charges are filed by prosecuting attorneys.

Many black citizens are being unjustly assaulted and physically abused by offending police officers, with no accountability. Many of these incidents of improper and abusive use of force, including murder, have been captured on cell phones and other recording devices. These images leave little doubt about what actually occurred. However, it seems that justification, acceptance, and disinterest in justice are the call of the day. When police officers shoot and kill unarmed citizens, how can they justify their actions? How much God can they have within when they maliciously beat or fatally injure someone who poses no threat to their safety and well-being? How much God can prosecuting attorneys have within themselves when they coldly ignore acts that are clear violations of the law by police officers and fail to prosecute these officers and uphold the law they swore to enforce?

During my thirty-three years in law enforcement, I worked various assignments and was promoted to various ranks. During my tenure in the Detroit Police Department, I was given many demanding and dangerous assignments, including precinct patrol, gang enforcement, homicide, and the Carjacking Task Force. Although I find the current climate of law enforcement and the unnecessary shooting and killing of African American citizens quite disturbing, I must acknowledge that, unfortunately, this is nothing new. Advancements in technology have led to capturing these shootings on video, which has finally exposed what has been going on in law enforcement for many decades, highlighting the long history of unjustified force and murder of black Americans.

I believe that the vast majority of police officers are honorable and committed to treating all citizens fairly and equitably. My purpose in writing this book is to provide an insider's perspective on the bad apples in law enforcement who are destroying the trust and confidence of citizens in this honorable profession. I will provide controversial but necessary solutions to combat the adverse actions of wayward police officers, to keep them from continuing their dishonorable service. This distrust and eroding confidence must be turned around in order to restore honor and dignity to the police profession.

2

WHY BLACK PEOPLE
DISTRUST THE POLICE

*"Because the poor are plundered and the
needy groan, I will now arise," says the
LORD. "I will protect them from those
who malign them." (Psalm 12:5)*

Abuse of Force

WHY DO SO MANY BLACK people distrust the police? Abuse
of force is at the top of the list. During these turbulent times, the
conduct of racist, rogue police officers has been widely exposed by
technological advances, particularly cell phone cameras and police
body cameras.

This technology has prevented police officers from covering up
despicable, improper uses of force and deters the use of catchphrases
historically used by police officers to justify their abusive behavior.
Technology has clearly exposed numerous unjust actions of police

officers nationwide, including the murder and shooting of unarmed black people.

Many abuse-of-force incidents have been televised nationwide and abroad, receiving major media attention. On March 3, 1991, the unjust beating of Rodney King by white police officers in Los Angeles was captured on video and received worldwide attention. Rayshard Brooks, Daniel Prude, Atatiana Jefferson, Botham Jean, Philando Castile, Alton Sterling, Freddie Gray, Eric Garner, Tamir Rice, Akai Gurley, and Michael Brown were all unarmed when they were killed by the police.

On May 25, 2020, George Floyd was murdered on camera by a white police officer in Minneapolis, Minnesota; the news received worldwide attention. These incidents resulted in demonstrations across America by disenfranchised black citizens; in the case of George Floyd, there were demonstrations worldwide.

There have been many other major incidents of abuse of force by white officers not caught on camera, such as the March 13, 2020, fatal shooting of Breonna Taylor, who was unarmed in her home in Louisville, Kentucky, and the November 5, 1992, murder of Malice Green, who was beaten while unarmed by white Detroit police officers.

Black citizens have been targets of this abuse nationwide, for much too long. Further, police departments have a long history of failing to hold their officers accountable for abusive actions. Today, mistrust of the police is at an all-time high, and there is greater awareness of abuse and unjust force perpetrated by law enforcement officers. Black civil rights groups have been protesting for decades, but the unjust abuse of black people continues to occur at the hands of mostly white police officers.

Lack of Police Accountability

A major factor that fuels black people's mistrust of police officers and police departments nationwide is the lack of accountability when officers use excessive force against black people. This lack of accountability is perpetrated by police chiefs, police unions, and prosecutors.

Police unions use their vast political power and influence to deter accountability. Their political action committees have monetary resources set aside for contributions to the campaigns of prosecutors, mayors, city council members, governors, and state representatives. Wielding this influence has proven to be quite effective in protecting police officers who use abusive force against black people.

Police chiefs have sided with police unions by failing to hold officers accountable. Most police chiefs are at-will employees who serve at the pleasure of the mayor, city manager, or city council. Some chiefs fall prey to police unions political power in order to protect themselves and their employment. If the police unions feel that the chief is not supporting their members, they will launch a campaign to have the chief removed. This is why reform-minded police chiefs do not last long and cannot make the necessary significant changes needed in problem police departments.

Prosecutors contribute to the black community's mistrust of police officers by siding with officers who use excessive force. Prosecutors have consistently failed to charge and prosecute police officers who cross the line. In many states, prosecutors have the final say in whether or not to charge police officers.

Police endorsements and contributions may also play a part because prosecutors are elected officials who work closely with police departments, a significant support base. This unwavering support for abusive police officers and lack of accountability have created an atmosphere of disgust, futility, and suspicion in black communities across the country.

Racial Profiling and Stereotyping

Racial profiling and stereotyping are another significant factor in black peoples' distrust of the police. On many occasions, young black men are stopped and investigated simply because of the color of their skin, the type of car they are driving, or the area of the city they are traveling in.

I too have been a victim of racial profiling and stereotyping, dating back to my teenage years. Growing up in Detroit, I was blessed to have five fantastic sisters. My three older sisters were women with professional jobs. Dr. Geneva Napoleon Smitherman was a professor at Wayne State University in Detroit, Bobby Napoleon White (MSW) was a supervisor in the State of Michigan's Department of Social Services, and Anita Napoleon was trainer for the Detroit Department of Transportation. They were very generous with allowing their younger brothers to drive their cars. When I was seventeen years old, I vividly remember driving my sister's Cadillac through the city to my grandfather's house on the East Side of Detroit. That day, I was stopped five times by different white police officers. I did not commit any traffic violations or crimes. Each time I was stopped, police officers searched me, my vehicle, and my trunk. They never explained the reason for the stop or why I was being searched. While they were searching my car, one police officer asked me, "Where are the drugs?"

I advised them that I didn't sell drugs.

The officer then stated, "Oh, you must be a pimp then."

All black men who drive Cadillacs are not drug dealers or pimps. This experience was demeaning and unnecessary. I had not committed any violation of the law. I was never issued a ticket during any of these encounters with the police.

In the early 1970s, while reading meters for Detroit Edison, I was racially profiled at least two times a week and investigated by the police. I was assigned to work in the white suburbs, where I was regularly stopped by the police. Even though I was wearing a company uniform, each time I was stopped by the police, I had to produce my company identification card and driver license. People must have been scared of the big afro I was wearing.

On one occasion, an officer asked me, "Couldn't your boss assign you to Detroit, instead of out here?"

I advised the officer that I had no control over assignments. As demeaning as this was, I did not file a complaint. Back when I was growing up, black people very seldom filed complaints against the police in order to keep the drama and trauma of the police out of their lives. As a people, we felt we had no voice; there was nobody to address our concerns, especially in the suburbs.

In 1985, my brother Benny Napoleon, former Detroit police chief and Wayne County sheriff, and I were racially profiled in Redford, Michigan, a suburb that borders Detroit. At that time, Benny was a lieutenant in the Detroit Police Department, and I was a police officer. We were going to pick up our tuxedos for Benny's upcoming wedding. He had just bought a brand-new Corvette convertible. We drove down Grand River Avenue in Redford with the top down. It was a beautiful sunny day, a perfect day to have the top down. We went into the tuxedo store and tried on our tuxedos for fitting. After leaving the store, we were driving down Grand River when a Redford police car behind us activated their lights and siren. Benny pulled his Corvette over, and the officer exited his vehicle. As the officer started walking up to the driver's side door, he pulled out his gun.

Benny could see the officer, and he advised me that he had his gun out. My brother placed his hands on the top of the steering wheel, and I placed my hands on the dashboard. When the officer got closer, he asked for Benny's driver license, registration, and proof of insurance. Benny told the officer that he was a lieutenant in the Detroit Police Department and that he was armed. The officer then pointed his weapon at both me and Benny. Benny told him that we both were police officers. However, the officer kept pointing his weapon at us.

Benny then asked the officer, "Can I show you my identification without you pointing your gun at us or shooting us?"

The officer kept saying he needed to see some ID while still pointing his gun at us. Finally, Benny advised the officer that his identification was in his right rear pocket, and that he would slowly take it out and show it to him. Benny took his police badge and identification and showed it to the officer, who was still pointing his weapon at us. The officer stated he still needed to see Benny's driver's license and registration and proof of insurance. Benny asked the officer to stop pointing his weapon at us, and the officer replied, "No."

Slowly, Benny took his driver's license, registration, proof of insurance, and department identification card and handed them all to the officer. But even after he gave the officer all these documents, he continued to point his weapon at us while looking at Benny's cards. He returned the documents to Benny but was still pointing his weapon at us.

Benny asked him what he stopped us for.

The officer stated that there was a robbery in the area, and our vehicle fit the description. He then turned toward his vehicle, put his gun back in his holster, got back into his car, and drove off. We sat there for a few minutes, reflecting on what just happened. We were very pissed off by the way the officer treated us. He had so little respect for us and would not stop pointing his gun at us, despite Benny providing his police identification to him. I said that someone that scared should not be working as a police officer because he would get somebody hurt or killed. We did not report the incident to the Redford Police, because we believed that no action would be taken against the officer.

Black women are also victims of racial profiling and stereotyping. Many young black women are disrespected and demeaned at bus stops while waiting for the bus. Many police officers have accused innocent women of being prostitutes simply because they were waiting for the bus to arrive. Many black women are unjustly ticketed for loitering while waiting at the bus stop. This blatant misconduct and disrespect for black women by police officers should not be tolerated.

It is also painful and scary to know that while racial profiling usually doesn't lead to injury or death, there is always a chance that such an incident could horrifically escalate. When a black man encounters police, he often has to worry that the officer might kill or injure him, even if he has done nothing wrong.

Such encounters with police and the resulting fear are far less common for whites. Widespread racial profiling also poisons relationships between police and minority communities. This is the reality that black people in America go through on a daily basis. I thank God that I had a mother and father who taught me how to survive the police while growing up in Detroit. My parents taught me to never be disrespectful to or argue with police officers, keep your hands where officers can see them, give them what they ask for, and never reach for anything without first asking.

Disparity in Enforcement

It has been unequivocally proven that there is a tremendous racial disparity in the enforcement of laws. This disparity is glaring and occurs throughout America. You only have to observe traffic court in almost any municipality to see this disparity.

Using information obtained through public record requests, the Stanford Open Policing Project examined almost 100 million traffic stops conducted from 2011 to 2017 across twenty-one state patrol agencies, including California, Illinois, New York, and Texas, and twenty-nine municipal police departments, including New Orleans, Philadelphia, San Francisco, and St. Paul, Minnesota. The results show that police stopped and searched black and Latino drivers on the basis of less evidence than used in stopping white drivers, who are searched less often but are more likely to be found with illegal items. The study does not conclude that officers knowingly engaged in racial discrimination. Rather, its nuanced analysis of traffic stop data establishes the fact that race is a factor when people are pulled over by police and that this behavior is occurring across the country.

Lack of Diversity

The lack of diversity in police departments nationwide is problematic for the black community. Many people in black communities have an extremely difficult time trusting police officers and departments because the citizens in these communities have been abused and treated unfairly by white officers. The black community feels that they don't have an avenue of support when they only see white supervisors who are charged with investigating those officers who abuse and mistreat them.

Police departments nationwide must reflect the pluralistic makeup of their communities to gain the trust of all their citizens. Racial diversity must be reflected in all ranks of the police department. If not, the community will continue to suffer and lose trust in their police department.

Historical Abuse

Historical abuse perpetrated against black people in America by mostly white police officers is undeniable. This abuse was clearly documented during the Civil Rights movement under the leadership of Dr. Martin Luther King Jr. Countless film footage exists documenting the violence perpetrated against black citizens during peaceful protest. In nearly every case, the police initiated the violence, even though black citizens had the right to peaceful assembly. There is undisputable evidence that many of the police officers abusing black citizens during the Civil Rights era were members of the Ku Klux Klan, a white supremacist terrorist organization that has been allowed to operate for decades.

According to an article written in *DiversityInc* dated July 21, 2014, two Florida police officers, a deputy chief and police officer, lost their jobs after an FBI informant claimed they were members of the Ku Klux Klan. Both officers were identified as members of the Ku Klux Klan by the Klan's Grand Dragon in Florida. The FBI did a great job of destroying the Black Panther organization but has done very little to disrupt the Ku Klux Klan.

During civil disturbances, innocent black citizens have been abused or killed by police officers. Black people have been abused by the police since the formation of the first police departments in America. The disparity in enforcement, the murder of black citizens, the mental and physical abuse by police officers, the failure to hold the police accountable for criminal violations—this is what magnifies the distrust of police departments by black citizens nationwide. This historical abuse of black citizens has understandably created a wall of distrust between the black community and police departments.

3

A COURSE IN SURVIVAL

Finally, be strong in the Lord and in the
strength of his might. (Ephesians 6:10)

THE TITLE OF THIS CHAPTER originates in my personal conviction about humanity and my professional experience in law enforcement. I sincerely and wholeheartedly believe that every person has a right to live. From my many years of serving and protecting humanity, I know firsthand how dangerous the job of policing is; police must make quick decisions to protect their lives and defend the lives of others. However, in those instances where police officers abuse their authority and misuse their power, citizens' lives are far too often at risk. It is those citizens for whom I've written this chapter.

Although I title this chapter "A Course in Survival," I'm not suggesting that all cops are out to kill people. What I am saying is that too many officers have not been properly vetted or trained to diffuse a situation to accomplish the most significant outcome for everyone involved: life.

Only someone who is completely disconnected from society or lives in constant denial would argue that police brutality is not a crucial matter in America. Given the technology of police body cameras and citizens' cell phone videos, the unjustified use of police brutality and misconduct can no longer be swept under the rug. Our society is now experiencing a backlash of demonstrations from social justice groups in nearly every major city in America.

Although I am now retired, my resolve will always remain the same as when I was a police officer, sergeant, lieutenant, and police chief: to protect and serve people. That is my calling. I want you to live, not die. My purpose in this chapter is to provide you with tools and common-sense strategies to increase your chances of survival if you are confronted with an officer who refuses to follow proper protocol or is blatantly racist.

A Different Culture

Let's look at how American society and culture have changed from my grandfather's and my father's time in the 1940s to today in 2021. My father, Reverend Harry Nelson Napoleon, was born in Tennessee, to a black man (also named Harry) and a black mother. However, this black man, Harry Napoleon Sr., my grandfather, had a Caucasian father and an African American mother. My father's mother died in childbirth, and he grew up in the household of his Caucasian grandfather and his African American father. It was the era of a racially terroristic deep South, and both my father and my grandfather were exposed to every facet of segregation, Jim Crow laws, brutality, and violence visited upon black men by Southern whites. In my father's book, *The Life and Legend of Louis ("LOU")*

Napoleon, he describes some of his experiences with racism and brutality visited upon black men:

> When I was seventeen years old, I left Tennessee because I didn't like the way White people treated Black people. We would go to Brownsville on Saturdays, but we couldn't stay in town past 9:00 p.m. The police would drive into the Black part of town and blow their whistles for us to leave town at 9:00 p.m. If you didn't leave, they would come back a second time, blowing their whistles and saying, "Niggers, when we come back, we better not see a nigger nowhere. If we do, we are going to start whipping asses and putting you in jail." I didn't like that, and I told my father if any White man ever hit me, I was going to kill him and my daddy thought I would do it. He thought I would try to do what he was doing. He wouldn't back down from any of them, but the Whitehurst's were protecting him. If not for that protection, the Whites would have killed him.

Here is another excerpt from *The Life and Legend of Louis ("LOU") Napoleon:*

> When I left Brownsville, it was a few months after the Klan had lynched Elbert Williams in April, 1940. They went to Elbert Williams' house late one night. The man that Elbert worked for, Mr. Dupree, knocked on his door and stated his name. When Elbert opened the door, Charles Reed, the police officer, stepped in, and Elbert saw Mr. Dupree and asked, "Mr. Dupree what's wrong? Did something happen at the cleaners?" Mr. Dupree didn't answer

or say a word. Elbert said to Charles Reed, "I'm in my pajamas; let me get my clothes on." Charles Reed said, "Come on, let's go; you may not need no damn clothes." They took him to the Hatchet [Tallahatchie] River bridge, cut off his genitals, tied them around his waist, shot him eleven times, and threw him over the bridge into the Hatchet River.

Elbert Williams was lynched because he was trying to organize the NAACP in Haywood County, Brownsville, Tennessee. After he was lynched, the County Sheriff had a Mexican stand-off with some of the Ku Klux Klan mob. He went by himself to the river with the undertaker to pick up Elbert Williams body. Sheriff Hawkins was a good Sheriff. All the Black people liked him. After he retrieved Elbert's body, he resigned from being Sheriff because he was so angry about the lynching. That was enough for me. I didn't want to live their anymore. So, I left. My White grandfather cried like a baby. I was his only grandchild. He and my father wanted to give me money, but I refused to take it. I told them I could make my own way and left home with only $6.00 in my pocket.

Coincidentally, I had my own encounter with hostile racism and bigotry in my grandfather and father's home state of Tennessee, while a member of the Kentucky State University baseball team. In May of 1975, we were playing in the regional final of the National Association of Intercollegiate Athletics baseball tournament in Nashville. We were playing the host college team in the championship game. Because we were playing the host team, there was a very large crowd at the game, approximately twenty-five hundred people. At that time, this was the largest crowd our team ever played before. From the start of the game to the very end, the crowd did everything they could to intimidate our team. Kentucky State University was a historical black college, and our baseball team consisted of predominantly black players with two white teammates, and our opponent was all white players. Our team was unique in that twenty of the twenty-five players came from inner-city high schools in Detroit. White colleges up North gave few, if any, baseball scholarships to black baseball players. All of the Kentucky State players from Detroit were outstanding athletes and made the All-City baseball teams in the Detroit Public School Baseball League.

Throughout the game, the people in the crowd sitting directly behind our bench called us every black racist slur imaginable. They called us niggers, coons, burr heads, porch monkeys, jungle bunnies, spearchuckers, watermelon eaters, half-men, ghetto dwellers, and other slurs I can't remember. They even used racist slurs towards our two white teammates. They called them nigger lovers and nigger-loving hillbillies. They escalated their intimidation tactics by throwing small pebbles on our backs while seated on the players' bench. The crowd did not try to injure us, but to aggravate and intimidate us.

I became worried because I could see in the faces of some of my teammates that they were angry and upset at how we were being treated. Because of my upbringing and own experiences with racism, I advised my teammates that we could not respond to their ignorance and hatred. I told them to stay together and get through this. This was the first time any of us experienced this type of racism at this level and intensity. I was proud of my teammates for the way they conducted themselves under such trying circumstances. Things could have been disastrous if we responded negatively.

The game was close; we lost but were relieved to be going back to our hotel rooms. After the game, an elderly white man and his wife came on our bus and apologized for the way we were treated. He told us he was embarrassed and ashamed of the conduct of all spectators who used racist and abusive language towards us, saying it should not have happened.

Under theses austere conditions, survival was every black person's concern. One way for blacks to survive was by being subservient and extra respectful to whites. Although that didn't always work, it worked more times than it didn't. "Yes sir, no sir. Yes ma'am, no ma'am": This was common vernacular for black people. We were taught how to talk to people, respect our elders, and not to be confrontational, especially with people in authority. Being aggressive could cost you your life. Most of us viewed that as entirely unnecessary and foolish. Some African Americans identified that approach as a "Bow down, get ran over" approach to life. Not me; I saw it then and still see it now as a common-sense approach to living a long life.

I come from a solid, dignified heritage. We were raised to go the long haul, fall in love, raise a family, and contribute to society. My family believed in the American dream, and we wanted to live a long, prosperous life. Dying because of an argument that could have been averted didn't make sense to my people. If you can create a peaceful outcome, do so. That's my motto.

Unfortunately, today, many of our young people, both black and white, are being raised in fatherless homes, single-parent households without the much-needed reinforcement to strengthen the family unit and teach children the consequences of their actions. Not having direction and discipline in the home is why so many young people have no idea how to speak appropriately, respect others, diffuse tense situations, or submit to authority when required. I saw respect demonstrated every day of my life by my dad. If we didn't display proper respect for people, we'd be properly punished. There were always consequences for bad behavior. Being raised with implications for behavior made us think about everything we did. We thought it through, realizing that we were going to pay now or later for whatever we did.

Today, few kids are taught to show proper respect for people, which puts them at high risk for getting into a negative situation with law enforcement. I've often experienced young men acting extraordinarily disrespectful and rude, swearing, and totally obnoxious. Unfortunately, this can be a perfect storm that creates a deadly situation with the wrong police officer. I've seen a lot in my thirty-three years of policing. I've been personally insulted, called a "pig," sworn at, and even threatened. Because I know the people I policed, I recognized their behavior as a gross lack of home training, and it did not faze me. In some ways, I felt compassion for them, realizing that their behavior directly resulted from a lack of structure and often love in their lives. While it was disrespectful and rude, I didn't get offended when they went off on me. My line has long been, "We can do this one of two ways, the easy way or the hard way. Which way do you want to do this?"

I give them options, even when they're out of control. Why is that? It's because I don't want to hurt anyone; I most definitely don't want to take anybody's life. However, if a person is out of control and poses a threat to my life, I'm left with very few options for resolving the situation peacefully. Often, I'll say, "Listen, let's talk this out." In most cases, my peaceful approach tends to calm the perpetrator down.

In the case of a traffic violation, I immediately tell drivers why I pulled them over. Some officers don't like to tell citizens why they pulled them over, but they are required to do so by most police departments. A red flag is when you have an officer who pulls you over for a traffic stop but refuses to inform you why. In fact, that's one of the main reasons why police officers get in trouble in traffic stops. They fail to follow protocol.

If you believe that an officer has not followed proper steps in doing their job, there are some things you should do and other things you shouldn't do if you want a favorable outcome. Let's take a look.

Do Not Do!

1. Do not be confrontational.

    Let's face it. We were all made with varying temperaments. Some people are incredibly patient, peaceful, and agreeable. Others live for a fight and always want to argue and disagree. You can even observe these varying degrees of behavior in your own family. The point is that everybody is different. Some people are more prone to fly off the handle than others. Cops are no different. You have super patient officers who always seek peace. Others, not so much. If you come face to face with an officer who is easily disturbed, being confrontational is the number one way to cause a situation to grow totally out of control. Try not to confront a police officer when stopped or even arrested. Doing so won't make it better for you. As best as you can, try to listen to the officer, hear what he is asking for, and work with him for best results.

2. If you are pulled over, make sure that you keep your hands in sight so the officer won't feel threatened.

    Understand that police officers may think that you are reaching for a weapon. Since they are required to take the greater risk, they have to protect themselves. That's no justification for killing somebody because you mistake an iPhone for a Glock. Nonetheless, this is about protecting you. So don't give officers any reason to think you may cause them harm.

3. Don't put passengers in unnecessary danger.

    You have to be mindful of people in the car with you who have nothing to do with you being pulled over. Be extra careful if you have people in your vehicle, as their behavior or attitude can create suspicion.

4. Be careful not to use profanity.

    In some cities and counties, cursing at an officer is a misdemeanor and can get you a ticket or even arrested. Furthermore, your foul language will only intensify the situation rather than diffuse it.

5. Never put your hands on a police officer.

    You are never allowed to put your hands on an officer. That's an assault. You will be arrested. Unless officers have a personal relationship with you, they have no idea what you may do. When you put your hands on them, it can be misinterpreted. Follow old-school advice, and keep your hands to yourself.

6. Stop trying to be your own lawyer.

    I've seen this way too many times. When you're stopped, respectfully ask why you were stopped. You are within your rights to do so. If you're arrested, ask why you're being arrested. But unless you are a licensed attorney, don't try to be a lawyer in front of the officers; they won't be impressed with your legal knowledge. When you have your day in court, you'll have ample time to defend yourself, as you are allowed to do so by law. If you insist on trying to be your attorney, the officer may become upset.

To Do

1. Try your best to cooperate.

    I know this doesn't always work. I also realize that, unfortunately, people have been murdered even while being compliant. Those are some of the saddest situations ever and are inexcusable. However, in many situations, a favorable outcome occurs simply because people cooperated. As best as possible, please cooperate and believe in promising results.

2. If you feel an officer has wronged you or acted illegally in your situation, report it to a police supervisor.

Understand that good chiefs of police do not want bad things unreported. Most police chiefs are good, honest, upstanding people who want to run an aboveground department. They don't want bad cops on their force. They want to know who is operating poorly so they can quickly deal with them. People say, "If I report it, they're not going to do anything about it anyway." That's not true. While you may not get the immediate result that you want, the fact that you filed a report is a good thing because that goes on the officer's record and stays there as a reference point. If you say nothing, we will never know, and what we don't know, we can't correct. More than that, if people never report them, those officers will continue to get away with doing wrong things, possibly criminal activity toward their victims. File your complaint. It's the right thing to do.

When Police Officers Abuse Their Position

Few people know what to do when police officers overstep their authority or abuse their position. For example, many people are unaware that if a driver is pulled over for a routine traffic stop, the passengers in the car are not required by law to identify themselves if they've not been involved in any unlawful actions. Only the driver is required to present identification to the officer.

However, let me add that I've asked people for their information who were traveling with a driver. I did so because good officers keep a log to develop sources of information. In many cases, by identifying yourself to officers, it can help you to be treated more favorably, particularly when they realize you were not involved in any unlawful conduct.

Here are a few things that are abuses of an officer's authority.

1. Excessive force. An officer is never allowed to use excessive force when dealing with any citizen. Excessive force is always considered an undue influence. For example, if a suspect is unarmed, shooting that person is considered using excessive force.

2. Unnecessary force. Beating a person mercilessly who has not shown themselves as a threat to an officer's safety is a disproportionate use of force and is not allowed.

3. When an officer refuses to tell you why you've been stopped or why you've been arrested, that officer has acted improperly. You are entitled to know why you are being stopped, detained, or arrested. It's your right, and it's the law.

4. Criminal sexual misconduct. An officer cannot request sexual favors in exchange for releasing a suspect. That is illegal and can result in jail time for the officer.

5. Officers are never allowed to take money as payment for a ticket, warning, or release from an arrest. Bribes are illegal and, under some circumstances, constitute a federal crime.

6. Unless officers are in a legitimate life-threatening situation, they are not allowed to pull their gun. Far too often, officers are the ones who cause confrontation, and then problems escalate out of control. When that happens, know that the officer is in the wrong; remain peaceful, and once released, be sure to file the appropriate complaint concerning the officer's misconduct.

Let me level with you: Officers who are sworn to protect and serve should always do what's right. However, as humans, people don't always do the right thing. I've laid out these recommendations as a means to protect your life.

People shouldn't have to stick their hands out of the car to ensure an officer's safety, but they do. It is what it is. Until protocols change, and until criminals no longer exist in our society, we'll have to do what's needed to protect ourselves and the people we love. For me, being alive is always better than being right.

4

ACUTE JUSTIFICATION SYNDROME

The wicked plot against the righteous and gnash their teeth at them. (Psalm 37:12)

ACUTE JUSTIFICATION SYNDROME (AJS) IS a phrase I coined after consistently witnessing police departments attempt to justify poor decision-making and misconduct perpetrated by bad police officers. AJS is the unrighteous support of misconduct by police officials; it happens nationwide, and it is supported by many police chiefs, prosecutors, and district attorneys. Some police chiefs utilize AJS to gain the favor and support of their officers. Other police chiefs strategically employ AJS in their quest for political office. It enables them to gain favor with voters supportive of the police.

The major perpetrators of AJS are leaders and members of

police unions. The mindset of unions is to protect their members at all times and at all cost, regardless of the damage to the image and reputation of the police department. Union leaders have gone so far as to assist police officers with their reports to ensure they do not record anything that could be used against them. AJS is most prevalent in the use of fatal and improper force against African Americans and other people of color. No matter how egregious the officer's actions, AJS syndrome allows unions to protect bad officers, to have their backs.

AJS involves carefully contemplated and skillfully crafted defense mechanisms to justify an officer's actions. These mechanisms include the use of historic law enforcement catchphrases, such as, "I was in fear of my life," "He made a furtive gesture," "I thought that he had a weapon," "I felt my life was in danger," "He was reaching for a weapon," "The public was in danger," and "He had a shiny object in his hand." These phrases have been used throughout history, resulting in police officers avoiding prosecution for abusive treatment and use of force on innocent citizens.

"I feared for my life" is the most popular AJS tool used by police officers in cases involving fatal force. The second most popular AJS tool used by police officers is, "He was reaching." As reported in the news article, "Shooting of Terrance Crutcher in Tulsa, Oklahoma" (Wikipedia.org), Officer Betty Jo Shelby, who is white, used the popular AJS tactic "He was reaching for something," when she shot and killed unarmed Terrance Crutcher during a stop for a traffic violation. What makes this incident so woeful is that there were three other police officers at the location, and two officers hovering above in a police helicopter when Officer Shelby killed Crutcher. Video camera footage shows Crutcher with his hands on top of his car when he was shot. None of the other officers fired their weapon. After the shooting was determined a homicide, the Tulsa County District Attorney charged Shelby with first-degree manslaughter. On May 17, 2017, a jury found her not guilty.

The officer's AJS defense was successful, and another black family was denied justice in the callous, brutal murder of their loved one.

Another tactic in AJS is vilification of victims of unwarranted police force by exposing negative factors in the victim's background. This includes such actions as the police leaking negative information to the media and public, such as the victim's criminal history. This strategy enables officers to garner community support to vindicate their abusive actions. This strategy can influence members of the public who may be seated as jurors to decide an officer's guilt or innocence.

A case in point is the murder of Malice Green in 1992 in the city of Detroit. Two Detroit police officers, Walter Budzyn and Larry Nevers, beat Green to death by striking him in the head seven to twelve times with a steel flashlight. Malice Green's previous criminal history was leaked to the media. In "25 Years ago, Malice Green became the Face of Police Brutality in Detroit," a *Detroit Free Press* article written by Elisha Anderson on November 3, 2017, Green had prior encounters with police, including an incident where he pleaded guilty to drunken driving and attempting to flee police and another where he pleaded guilty to battery on an officer. According to Marco Magaritoff's article in *All That's Interesting* entitled "The Brutal Story of Malice Green's Murder by Detroit Police," Green's arrest record included drunk driving on July 3, 1989, and trying to flee a squad car by kicking its door. He was accused of hitting his wife later that year and convicted in May 1990 of pushing two officers who answered yet another domestic abuse call. None of the prior incidents had anything to do with an unarmed Malice Green being beaten to death by two angry, tainted police officers. Both Budzyn and Nevers had checkered pasts, with numerous lawsuits, citizens' complaints, and excessive use of force complaints.

On August 23, 1993, the jury found Budzyn and Nevers guilty of second-degree murder. Two months later, Nevers was sentenced to twenty-five years in prison and Budzyn was sentenced to serve a lighter sentence of eighteen years in prison. However, because of

AJS defense mechanisms, both sentences were overturned because the movie, *Malcolm X*, was shown to the jury while they waited to begin deliberating. The movie's opening scenes show video of the Rodney King incident, which the court ruled was prejudicial. The effectiveness of AJS cannot be underestimated or dismissed.

Officer Budzyn was retried, and on March 19, 1998, he was again found guilty of involuntary manslaughter, and in January 1999, the Michigan Court of Appeals reinstated his four-year prison sentence. He had already served the minimum under the first conviction and was released.

Officer Nevers' 1997 appeal to the Michigan Supreme Court was denied. However, he was successful on his appeal to a federal court, which overturned the verdict in 1999. It cited the showing of *Malcolm X* as well as jury members' hearing of preparations in case of riots should the officers be acquitted. This decision was appealed to the US Supreme Court, which let it stand. In May 2000, Nevers was convicted of involuntary manslaughter and sentenced to seven to fifteen years in prison. In March 2003, this conviction was overturned by the Michigan Court of Appeals, but in September 2003, the Michigan Supreme Court upheld that conviction. In April 2005, Nevers lost a bid to appeal the conviction in federal court. During this process, Nevers was diagnosed with lung cancer, and he was released in 2001 to serve the rest of his sentence at home.

In the city of Minneapolis, a police officer placed his knee on the neck of a handcuffed George Floyd and choked him to death. Floyd's criminal history was released to the press.

According to the *Courier Daily News* article dated June 11, 2020, written by Sachin Jangra, entitled "George Floyd Criminal Past Record/Arrest History/Career Timeline: Baggie, Gun Pregnant and All Details," in 2009, George Floyd was arrested for a first-degree felony charge, as per police criminal records, for an armed robbery he took part in 2007; he spent five years in prison for breaking into a lady's house with the intent to rob her. His criminal record includes five convictions related to theft and possession and sale of cocaine. Floyd was arrested five times in twenty years; his last cocaine arrest dates back in 2005. He was also linked to two convictions in the 1990s for possession and theft of a controlled substance (cocaine). However, it is not clear whether or not Floyd served time in prison for this felony.

Floyd was convicted of a firearm robbery in August 1998, for which he served ten months at Harris County Jail. In April 2002, Floyd was condemned to thirty days of prison for trespassing on private property. He was involved in two more cocaine offenses, in October 2002 and in 2004, for which he served eight-month and ten-month sentences in prison, respectively. After another cocaine conviction in December 2005, Floyd served ten months in state jail. None of Floyd's prior incidents had anything to do with him being choked to death while unarmed and handcuffed on the ground by angry, tainted police officers. Further, the officer who choked Floyd had a checkered past, with numerous lawsuits, citizens' complaints, and excessive use of force complaints.

During my term of service as chief of police in Inkster, a use-of-force investigation revealed that an officer had struck a handcuffed prisoner without any reasonable justification. I conducted a chief's hearing, which resulted in the officer's termination. The police union, in a typical AJS performance, defended the conduct by stating that the prisoner was only struck one time and did not require medical attention. The union executives attempted to justify the officer's improper conduct on the grounds that the prisoner was not admitted to the hospital. I posed the counterargument that the union executives would not feel the same if the victim had been their wife, son, daughter, or someone they loved.

Another common AJS tactic is to use the medical examiner's report against victims killed by police officers. This report is a deceptive strategy to enhance police killing by exposing the medical deficiencies of the victim. This tactic was used in Detroit in the murder of Malice Green and in Minneapolis in the murder of George Floyd.

In the George Floyd case, Acute Justification Syndrome was on prominent display, with medical explanations that Floyd died of carbon monoxide poisoning, opioid abuse, heart failure, and other causes not even related to his actual cause of death, which was cardiopulmonary arrest, complicated by law enforcement restraint and neck compression, as reported by the medical examiner. All types of medical AJS excuses were offered up by the defense attorney to justify the officer's blatantly cruel attack. In many other cases throughout the country, this tactic has been commonly used on victims who were unjustly killed by police officers.

AJS syndrome is a destructive tool used to protect bad police officers and deceive the public about their actions. Those who perpetrate and support AJS knowingly and intentionally subvert justice. You cannot justify that which is unjustifiable. The main players who participate in AJS are the decision-makers: police chiefs, prosecutors, and police unions. In many instances, prosecutors have refused to issue warrants against police officers who unjustly kill citizens. This is what happened in Ferguson, Missouri, when the prosecutor refused to issue a warrant against the officer who shot and killed unarmed Michael Brown.

The perpetrators who use Acute Justification Syndrome are aware that most citizens view police officers in a positive manner. People see cops as heroes who protect them from danger on a daily basis. In the citizens' eyes, police officers risk their lives for the public they serve. These same citizens will be seated as jurors when a police officer is charged with a crime and placed on trial. Subconsciously, most citizens would like to believe that police officers would not be involved in any wrongdoing; they would grasp onto anything presented that would assist officers with their case. Perpetrators of AJS are well aware of citizens' sentiment toward police officers and are acutely aware of the AJS defense mechanisms that have been used effectively throughout history on behalf of police officers. They use these defense mechanisms to get a positive outcome for officers charged with serious offenses.

AJS has severely damaged the reputation of police departments and has resulted in a loss of faith in criminal justice in black communities nationwide. Time and time again, black citizens have died unjustly at the hands of wayward police officers who are not brought to justice. There cannot be two separate criminal justice systems in this country. America will not stand if it continues to allow injustice to go unpunished.

Jesus states in Mark 3:24, "If a kingdom be divided against itself, that kingdom cannot stand." Today, the kingdom of America is severely divided. Unless it lives up to its creed, "that all men and women are created equal," it will fall and wallow in its hate, racism, bigotry, deceit, and discrimination.

5

BAD COPS WILL LIE

These things do the Lord hate: A proud look, a lying tongue, and hands that shed innocent blood. (Proverbs 6:16–17)

THERE IS NOTHING MORE DISTURBING in the law enforcement profession than a police officer who does not tell the truth while enforcing the law. Lying must not be tolerated in any organization, especially the police department. Truthfulness must be maintained and is essential in order for police departments to survive and function in an orderly manner. Citizens expect their police officers to possess the highest degree of honesty, integrity, and truthfulness. These traits are extremely important to preserve the public trust in their law enforcement officers.

Police Officers who are found to be lying significantly destroys the public trust and faith citizens have in their police department. This destruction of public trust not only affects the local municipality, but affects cities and citizens nationwide. Many families nationwide have been seriously affected by untruthful officers who fabricate evidence, manipulate crime scenes, plant evidence, and who perjure themselves by giving false testimony under oath during criminal court proceedings.

Being framed and unjustly incarcerated by persons deceptively masquerading as police officers in a blue uniform with a badge, gun, and handcuffs is a travesty of justice. I believe that there are thousands of innocent people serving time in prison for crimes they did not commit. The Innocence Project supports this assertion. There is no room in law enforcement and the police profession for deceptive, false, misguided, self-serving police officers.

It must be stated the overwhelming majority of police officers are decent people, possessing honesty, integrity, and good character. However, some police departments across America employ some of the most deplorable, despicable, dishonest, untruthful, racist, human beings on the planet. These types of officer's cloak and disguise themselves in honor, dignity, intimidation, deception, distortion, and lies.

I know it is disappointing for citizens to hear these things about their police officers, but the truth must be told regarding the bad officers who dishonorably self-serve. Bad officers use the honorable office of police work to exercise their own self- serving personal preferences and agendas. They allow their personal prejudices and animosities to interfere with their obligation to properly and justly serve the entire community they swore to protect.

There was a time when it was hard for me to believe a police officer would lie to justify putting someone in jail. It was hard to believe until it happened to me. It happened to me while working as a police officer for the City of Detroit.

In March of 2005, I was on duty and assigned to the Fifth Precinct in the rank of Inspector. The rank of Inspector was an executive level position in the Detroit Police Department at that time.

As usual, the first thing I did when I started my work day was to review the massive amounts of paperwork that I receive on a daily basis. Most of the time when I finish reviewing and administering the paperwork, I would stop and change into my uniform. But I glanced up at the calendar and noticed it was getting close to my son's 25th birthday. My son was finishing his final year in law school. I was unsure whether I had to drop him from my medical insurance on his birthday, or if I could carry him on my insurance through the end of the year.

Sometime there is paperwork you have to prepare when removing children from your medical insurance coverage. Instead of changing into my uniform, I decided to go to police personnel wearing my civilian clothes. I got into my assigned unmarked police vehicle and started traveling toward the police personnel building.

The Fifth Precinct was located on the far east side of Detroit. Detroit Police Personnel was located on the northwest side of Detroit. Because of the distance, it was necessary to take the freeway, which was the fastest route to get to police personnel.

While merging onto westbound I-96 freeway, the traveling lanes merged from 4 lanes to 2 lanes because of extensive repaving of I-96. I was traveling in the far-right lane, traveling and moving with traffic at a speed of 55 MPH. Traffic was moderate at that time of the day, it was around 10:45 a.m. – 11:15 a.m.

As I was approaching the West Grand Blvd exit, I noticed a Michigan State Police vehicle sitting underneath the overpass. As I passed the Joy Road exit, I observed flashing lights in my rearview mirror of a Michigan State Police vehicle. I thought he was responding to an emergency and was trying to get past me. I pulled my vehicle over on the right shoulder in an attempt to allow the police vehicle to pass my vehicle. Instead of passing my vehicle, the State Police vehicle pulled directly behind my Detroit Police vehicle. I had an X plate on my vehicle, which is a designation for a city government municipal vehicle.

The officer approached my police vehicle and asked me for my driver license, registration, and proof of insurance. I advised the trooper I was a police officer and I was on duty. I showed him my badge and handed him my pictured Detroit Police Department identification card and my pictured State of Michigan driver license.

I opened the door to the glove box in my vehicle and showed the officer my police radio and attached microphone. After carefully examining my police identification card and comparing the information on my driver license, the officer returned my police identification card and driver license to me. The officer then went into one of the most disrespectful tirades I have ever experienced from a police officer.

The officer in a condescending and angry tone of voice asked me, "who do you think you are speeding in a construction zone". He asked me if I knew what the speed limit was in a construction zone. The officer continued his tirade for about 30 seconds. I advised the officer he had returned my credentials and far as I were concern, we were finished. I pulled back onto the freeway, leaving the officer in mid-sentence of his tirade. As I continued traveling on the freeway, I noticed the officer following my police vehicle with his oscillating lights flashing and siren blaring.

My exit was approaching, and I exited the freeway with the officer still following my police vehicle closely, with his lights and siren still blaring. I immediately pulled my vehicle over on the freeway service drive.

The officer exited his vehicle, approached my vehicle standing to the driver front side of my vehicle, with his hand on his holstered handgun. The officer advised me to get out of my vehicle because I was under arrest. Stunned by his demands, I responded to the officer, "for what"? The officer refused to tell me what I was under arrest for, and advised me again to get out of my vehicle because I was under arrest. I advised the officer he needed to call for his supervisor to come to the location, but he stated, "no you are under arrest". I advised the officer the 10th precinct was located on Livernois at Elmhurst and to meet me there to get the matter resolved. I started rolling up the window on my police vehicle when the officer rushed up to my door and attempted to place his hand inside my police vehicle. My window was nearly closed and the officer could not get his hand inside my vehicle. The officer then began vigorously pulling the door handle on my vehicle, with one hand on his holstered handgun, attempting to open my locked door. I drove my vehicle through the corner gas station to my right, fearing the officer would shoot at me. I turned right onto Livernois street and stopped at the red light. The officer pulled his vehicle directly behind my vehicle with his lights and siren on, with the radio microphone to his mouth.

The traffic signal changed and I drove my vehicle towards the 10th precinct with the officer following closely behind with the lights and siren on. Upon arrival at the 10th precinct, I parked my vehicle directly in front of the precinct. I exited and started walking towards the entrance to the 10th precinct. About three quarters the way to the precinct entrance door, the officer grabbed my arm and attempted to twist it behind my back to place me in handcuffs. I pulled away and stated I was not going to allow him to handcuff me, because we were at the precinct. As I got to the top of the porch, the officer placed his hand in the middle of my back, shoved me into the brick wall of the precinct, twisted my arm, and again attempted to handcuff me. I became very angry at the disrespectful way the officer was treating me. I had properly identified myself as a police officer, but this hateful, wayward, misguided officer assaulted me, and treated me without respect or dignity. My anger was trying to overcome me, but the holy spirit within me prevented me from retaliating against the officer.

I pulled away from the officer and told him I will not allow him to handcuff me. Officers from inside the precinct observed the struggle between me and the officer, and came outside and grabbed me. I was in plainclothes and the officer's who exited the precinct were not immediately aware I was a police officer until I verbally identified myself. The 10th precinct Inspector came outside, recognized who I was, and ordered the officers to release me. The officer told the Inspector I was under arrest. The Inspector replied, "not in this building he isn't". I entered the precinct and went directly to the Commander's office to advise him what transpired. After about three minutes, there were approximately four Michigan State Police vehicles that emerged in front of the precinct with lights and sirens blaring.

While in the Commander's office, I prepared a police report of the incident for Assault and, Battery against the officer. The officer had no valid reason to arrest me, no valid reason to place his hands on me, and no valid reason to use excessive force for shoving me into the brick wall.

After completing my police report, spiritual discernment came over me. Now you may be wondering, what is spiritual discernment? Spiritual discernment is a gift from GOD almighty that make known something that cannot be perceived by natural means. It allows you to be able to distinguish, discern, judge, or appraise a person, statement, situation, or environment. In this situation, my spiritual discernment was telling me that this officer was going to lie on me, and that I need to go directly to the Evidence Technician Unit to have my driver license and department identification card dusted for fingerprints to protect myself. As I was leaving the precinct, I noticed several news media vans approaching the precinct. I believed someone from the Michigan State Police contacted the media. I continued to the Evidence Technician Unit to put in a request to have my drivers license and police identification card processed.

When I returned home from work, the incident was the lead story on all the major television news stations in Detroit. The stations reported I was involved in a police chase with the Michigan State Police. I was astounded. I was wondering how could the media do a story without hearing from all involved persons. I was disappointed because I knew there was no police chase. The television media showed all those State Police vehicles camped in front of the 10th precinct, which appeared to bring some validity to their story. The next morning, the incident was the front- page story in both major newspapers. One of the headlines read, "Former Chief's Brother Involved in Chase with State Police". Once again, nobody from either newspaper contacted me for my side of the incident.

After I arrived for work the next day, I received a phone call from the Commander in the Chief's Office. I updated him to the truth as to what occurred between me and the state trooper. I explained there was no chase, I properly identified myself, and the information reported by the news media was not accurate or true. The Commander advised me the assault report I made against the officer will not be pursued by the department. He advised both agencies have to work together. However, it became evident the Michigan State Police did not feel the same way about working together. A few days after the incident, my brother, who was the former Detroit Police Chief, advised me the Michigan State Police submitted a felony warrant against me to the Wayne County Prosecutor Office. The State Police was requesting to charge me with Resisting and Obstructing a Police Officer and Fleeing and Eluding Police. I could not believe what I was hearing, but was not worried. I knew the officer would have to tell lies in his police report, and his own report will expose his lies. That's exactly what happened.

At the time I left the 10th precinct on the day of the incident, spiritual discernment came upon me. I did not understand at that time, what role my driver's license and police identification card would play regarding this incident. I trusted and obeyed my spirit, and it exposed the lies and omissions the officer would later tell in his police report.

I had the opportunity to review the officers police report. As expected, the circumstances were quite different from the truth of what actually happened. The officer lied in his police report. Proverbs 6:17 states, "GOD hates a lying tongue". All ungodly, racist police officers will eventually make mistakes that will expose their hatred, racism, lack of honesty, truthfulness, and integrity. Ungodly police officers do not have the protection and power of the holy spirit to guide and protect them making decisions. The officer stated the identification card I presented was defaced, which was not true. I still have my driver license and identification card from 17 years ago to prove the officer was not truthful. His report left out pertinent facts that would have exposed his erratic, questionable decision making and unjust actions. The officer would have an extremely difficult time explaining the following: (1) How could the officer say I was fleeing from him when I stopped for him three times; There were cameras on the freeway the first time I stopped, cameras at the gas station and McDonalds the second time I stopped, and cameras at the police station the third time I stopped that could document the three times I stopped; (2) How could the officer say I was fleeing from him, when I told him in advance where I was going, when I told him I was going to the 10th precinct; (3) How could the officer say I was fleeing from him, when I never varied my course of travel or turn onto any other street; (4) Why did the officer stop me the second time, after I presented proper identification the first time he stopped me on the freeway; (5) Why did the officer assault me at the precinct, after I properly identified myself as a police officer during the first stop on the freeway; (6) Why did the officer endanger the public by falsely announcing over his police radio he was involved in a vehicular chase, knowing the alleged vehicle was a police car occupied by a on-duty Detroit Police executive officer; (7) Why did the officer make numerous attempts to handcuff a on-duty police officer, knowing the officer identified himself?

Can you imagine a police officer lying on another police officer and preparing a false felony police report to try to unjustly send him to prison? Can you imagine if he did this to a police officer, how many innocent citizens he has done this to?

It is quite obvious the officer as well as Michigan State Police investigator mishandled this incident and had no interest in obtaining the TRUTH. The Michigan State Police investigator failed to interview me to get the TRUTH regarding this incident. The Wayne County Prosecutors Office dismissed the warrant request because it was not based on the TRUTH.

One of the most rewarding experiences of my police career was serving as the police chief of the Inkster Police Department. What made the experience most rewarding is that the citizens of Inkster, Michigan, were very supportive of my efforts during my four years there, where I maintained their safety and security under trying times. The city was on the verge of bankruptcy, and I had to lay off two-thirds of the police department. Despite all this, my relationship with the citizens was admirable, and they continued to support me in my efforts to keep them safe. However, my relationships with a small faction of dissident police officers and police unions were tenuous, at best.

The police officers in the Inkster police department were represented by two unions; one union represented the police officers, and the other union represented the police supervisors. This small faction of dissident police officers were mostly elected union officials who wanted to control the police department and impede my ability to properly provide police services to the community.

They attempted to undermine my authority by meeting with the city manager, who the police chief reports to, and providing him with false and untrue information. They further attempted to undermine my authority by writing letters and submitting false information to the mayor and city council members. The police unions and their members were not happy with the way I reorganized the police department after laying off 75 percent of the department. Both unions were unhappy that I disbanded the motorcycle unit and the special response team. These police officers were some of the most racist, self-serving, dishonest, and despicable liars I have ever worked with. They used their positions in the union as protection against any discipline that could be initiated against them. They submitted false statements as union complaints to protect themselves against disciplinary action (submitting union complaints makes it difficult to hold any one person accountable). They did not care whether the information was true or not. Through lying and deception, these officers attempted to get me fired by sending false information to the governor of Michigan, Inkster's mayor and city manager, the city council, newspapers, and television stations. These officers submitted false statements repeatedly in their attempts to discredit my competency, honesty, integrity, reputation, and character.

These officers prepared an eleven-page memorandum, falsely accusing me of being incompetent, ignorant, retaliatory, and incapable of running the department; showing favoritism; interfering with criminal investigations; endangering officers lives; disregarding the union contract; utilizing the petty cash fund to buy my lunch; failing to allow medical retirements; ordering officers back to work with medical conditions; improperly releasing prisoners; improperly returning firearms to citizens; failure to turn in receipts; poor decision-making; and many other unsubstantiated complaints. These officers failed to submit any documents, proof, or evidence to substantiate any of the allegations made against me in their memorandum. This memorandum was submitted to the governor, mayor, city manager, city council, newspapers, and television media. These officers' shameful accusations lacked truth and moral consciousness; they showed no regret, remorse, and humility. Their blatant arrogance and immeasurable ignorance severely compromised their honesty and eliminated their integrity, by submitting false, libelous, and slanderous rhetoric against the chief of police.

I conducted a complete and thorough investigation with

documented proof regarding the officer's false allegations. Documented proof means you provide documents that refute false allegations made against someone. This can be any type of documentation, whether internal police documents or memorandums, written rules and regulations, the police union contracts, or any other document that will refute false allegations made against someone. For instance, the unions falsely accused me of failing to allow medical retirements in their letter of complaint to the governor, city officials, and news media. I researched the Inkster city charter, which stated that medical retirements can only be approved or denied by the pension board. I provided a copy of this section of the city charter as documented proof that I could not have denied police medical retirements. I was not a member of the pension board; therefore, the unions allegations against me were demonstrably false.

I provided documented proof that I did not improperly release any prisoners, proof that I did not improperly release firearms to anyone, proof I did not utilize petty cash to buy lunch, proof I did not fail to allow medical retirements, proof I did not order officers back to work with medical conditions, proof I returned receipts regarding petty cash, and proof I did not interfere with criminal investigations. I provided documented proof on many other false allegations delineated in their memorandum.

I prepared a twenty-seven- page memorandum addressing each of the officer's false claims. I had to be the one to conduct the investigation, even though the allegations were made against me. Because of the size of the department, we had no internal affairs unit to conduct the investigation. Additionally, I knew what it would take to do an impartial investigation because of my training and experience. I provided undisputed, impartial evidence that the information provided by the unions was false and not truthful. I submitted my memorandum to the mayor, city manager, and city council. It should be noted that the governor did not respond to me or the officers regarding their memorandum. The major newspapers and television stations also did not respond to me or the officers regarding their memorandum.

On January 3, 2013, *The Ledger Star*, a small suburban newspaper with limited circulation, published an article with the headline, "Vote of 'No-Confidence' Filed by Unions against Inkster Police Chief." The newspaper took the side of the officers and printed the lies they wrote in their memorandum. One of the lies printed in the article was that I returned an unregistered firearm to someone, which was not the truth. The article stated that the Command Officers Union filed a unanimous vote of no-confidence against the Inkster chief with the city manager.

After reading the article, spiritual discernment came upon me. This discernment led me to focus on the unanimous vote of no-confidence alleged by the Command Officers Union. My spiritual discernment directed me to focus on the word "unanimous" and told me that not every officer voted against me. When people lie to you and have no God in them, they do not and cannot realize the shortcomings of their thought process. Proverbs 6:16–17 states that God hates liars. A lie cannot stand up to what is true, and all liars will be exposed.

I called a meeting with the Command Officers Union representative and ordered him to have all his members meet with me the next day. I ordered all members to tell me whether or not they participated in the vote of no-confidence. This made the union rep very uncomfortable, and he told me that what I asked his members to reveal was privileged information. I advised the union rep that what I asked was not privileged nor improper, because he was the one who violated the union contract and protocol by negotiating their grievances in the newspapers. The union rep said he needed to consult with the union attorney, and I granted his request. I advised all officers present to meet with me the next day after they consulted with their attorney.

The next day, I met with the union rep and his member officers and ordered them to tell me whether they participated in the vote of no-confidence. I advised them that I already knew how each one voted, because the article stated the vote was unanimous. The union rep interjected that they did not have to answer my inquiry. I then ordered everyone to sign a Garrity form. Garrity is a legal decision that requires police officers to answer questions by a superior officer, but can't be used in a court of law. After signing the Garrity forms, I advised the officers that if they refused to answer me, they would be terminated from the police department for insubordination; they could leave their badge, gun, and identification card on the table. All officers complied and answered my question, and their answers revealed only four officers voted; four others did not participate in the vote for various reasons. The union rep knowingly lied about me in the *Ledger Star* newspaper story. I advised the union rep that a misconduct report would be prepared against him for lying.

I prepared the misconduct report and submitted it to the city manager for review. After reviewing my report, the city manager decided to override my decisions to discipline the officers for lying. I told him he was making a big mistake by not allowing me to discipline these officers. The city manager said he believed it would be problematic if I disciplined the officers because it would look like I was retaliating against union officers expressing their grievances. I explained to the city manager that I clearly delineated in my investigation and provided supporting documents that substantiated the union officers lied and added that it would be problematic if he did not allow me to discipline the officers. I also advised the city manager that the rules of the Inkster Police Department and the collective bargaining agreement did not exclude union officers from being disciplined when violations are committed. However, the city manager reiterated his decision not to discipline the officers.

Citizens need to be made aware of and understand that the chief of police does not have the authority to make the final decisions regarding disciplining officers, in police departments whose officers are represented by unions. In most of these departments, the final decisions regarding disciplinary matters are made through arbitration or the Board of Police Commissioners.

I returned to my office, closed my door, sat down in my chair, and fell into deep contemplative wonderment of the decision made by the city manager. My spiritual discernment told me his decision was not good, but I could not convince the city manager to allow me to discipline the officers for lying. While I don't automatically assume that race is a factor in decisions made against me, undeniably race continues to be a reality in American society today. I concluded that the white city manager refused to allow the black police chief to discipline white police officers, who told numerous lies about the black police chief, who had undeniable evidence that the white officers submitted lies to the governor, mayor, city manager, city council, newspapers, and television media.

I tried to look at the city manager's reasoning and make some sense of his decision not to discipline these officers for lying. I wondered if the appearance of retaliation was more important than the reality and verification that police officers lied about me. After exiting my state of wonderment and contemplation, I documented the city manager's decision in writing, because my discernment told me that this incident would not be the end.

A few months after the police union officers' misguided (and unsuccessful) letter-writing campaign against me, the chief union steward filed a whistleblower civil lawsuit against me and the city of Inkster. He alleged in his lawsuit that I retaliated against him because he was the union steward, that I discriminated against him by not promoting him to sergeant, that I used intimidation and abusive language, and many other lies. He even used the eleven pages of lies he submitted to the governor as proof of his allegations. I met with the city manager and informed him of the lawsuit filed against me and the police department. As it turned out, the city manager's inability to allow me to discipline those officers became problematic to him, me, the police department, and the city of

Inkster. As usual, what my spiritual discernment was telling me became my reality.

On August 23, 2015, at the beginning of the whistleblower trial, I had an uneasy feeling that the chief union steward would tell lies about me. My certainty was based upon my awareness of how some police officers and union members treated the previous police chief by filing untrue lawsuits against him (which they won). I was also concerned about the makeup of the jury. The jury consisted of mostly women and one man, and I didn't think they could see through this officer's lies. I was hoping he would come to his senses and answer the questions truthfully. I was hoping that after taking the oath and swearing to tell the truth, the oath would mean something to him. Unfortunately, he continued to dishonor himself and disgrace the badge, and he continued lying under oath.

I became angry with all of the union steward's lying, and I had to be constantly mindful not to show my anger to the jury. At one point during the trial, the union steward broke down on the witness stand and started crying. I became completely exasperated. I glanced over at the jury and saw that his crying stunt completely won them over. I knew no matter what I said to defend myself, the jury was going to rule in his favor. The union steward followed up his fake crying performance by getting other police officers to falsely testify on his behalf.

Needless to say, I was livid. In my thirty-three-plus years as a police officer, I had never witnessed this much lying by police officers under oath. I began to feel sorry for them. The Bible clearly states that God hates a liar. I know that on Judgment Day, they will not be able to escape God's wrath. Just as I expected, the jury came back with a judgment in favor of the union steward in the amount of one hundred thousand dollars. All I could do was shake my head in disgust.

Bolstered by their success of the whistleblower lawsuit, union officers and their members continued their vendetta to get me fired.

They initiated a plan to notify the media that I was mismanaging the police department. The union officers provided the news media with a copy of an invoice regarding repairs that I had made to my department vehicle. Union officers told reporters that I would rather get my vehicle repaired than to provide toilet paper for the officers and prisoners, which was another lie. The news media ran the story on television, without contacting me to determine the validity of the information provided by lying police officers. I was working late and noticed someone walk into the police station and drop off a pack of toilet paper at the front desk area. Shortly thereafter, another person came into the station and dropped off toilet paper.

I asked the person, "Why did you bring toilet paper to the police station?"

She responded, "I saw on the news that Inkster Police needed toilet paper, and I just wanted to help the police with their toilet paper shortage."

I thanked her for her kindness and support but assured her that we had enough toilet paper. I returned to my office, got on my computer, and brought up the news stories regarding our alleged toilet paper shortage. The story had already been broadcast and the false information put out over the airways.

I checked the storage cabinet and observed that there were two and a half cases of toilet paper in the cabinet. I had one of my officers contact all the news stations to advise them that there was not a toilet paper shortage at the Inkster Police Department and requested that they discontinue to broadcast the story. When I returned to work the following morning, I walked by the control desk and noticed the chief union steward with a satisfied smirk on his face.

People who are reading this book must be wondering, "Why are these officers in an uproar against the chief of police?" The simple answer is money and control. Shortly after I became police chief, the city manager gave a budget presentation predicting a significant shortfall in revenues because of the reduction of state revenue sharing, two thousand home foreclosures, and a deficit in the water fund. Therefore, in order for the city to prevent bankruptcy, we had to make significant cuts in the budget. These budget cuts required me to lay off 75 percent of the police department, from eighty-three personnel and officers to twenty-five. Prior to the layoffs, I conducted an audit of the police officers time banks, and it revealed that officers were putting comp time hours in their banks that was not approved by me nor agreed to by the collective bargaining agreement. Subsequently, I removed all the unapproved time from their banks, which resulted in some of the most despicable behavior by police officers I ever witnessed during my entire career as a police officer, some of which is mentioned in this book. Now, on to something extremely important.

If you want to truly understand the problems of policing in America, you should read the story of Detroit Police Officer Raymond Peterson. This type of conduct by police officers is not just restricted to Detroit but permeates throughout police departments across America. These problems were documented in an article published by Detroit Under Fire, a project of the Policing and Social Justice History Lab, an initiative of the University of Michigan Department of History and U-M Carceral State Project entitled *In Focus: Raymond Peterson*:

> S.T.R.E.S.S. (Stop the Robberies Enjoy Safe Streets) was an undercover Detroit Police decoy unit formed in January of 1971 at the direction of Detroit Mayor Roman Gribbs and newly appointed Police Commissioner John Nichols. Street crimes were reaching ridiculous new levels, with a breath-taking jump of 25% in 1970, for over 21,000 street robberies reported in 1970. Furthermore, 69 of those robbery victims were murdered in 1970, with the majority of the victims being African American.

Raymond Peterson was the most notorious member of the STRESS unit and probably killed more civilians in separate incidents in a compressed time period than any other police officer in modern American history. During 1971 alone, the first year of the STRESS operation, Peterson's undercover decoy unit was responsible for eight fatal shootings and two additional non-fatal incidents. Raymond Peterson pulled the trigger in at least five of these homicides, all of African American males, all in suspicious circumstances, and fired his weapon in the rest as well. He offered no apologies for keeping the streets safe from "vicious people" and doing his part to maintain order in Detroit's low-income Black neighborhoods, which he considered to be *worse* than a "jungle."

Before he volunteered for the STRESS unit in 1971, Peterson had compiled a long track record of brutality toward African American citizens since joining the DPD in 1961 as a 25-year-old. This included the vicious beating of Barbara Jackson in 1964, which the DPD covered up until the Michigan Civil Rights Commission found Peterson responsible for violating her civil and constitutional rights in a landmark ruling. Instead of removing Peterson from the force and charging him with felony assault, the Detroit Police Department issued a mild "reprimand" and kept him on the streets. Patrolman Peterson received at least twenty more excessive force complaints from residents of Detroit over the next six years but managed to stay out of the news until September 1971, when the civil rights investigations of STRESS that followed the deaths of Ricardo Buck and Craig

Mitchell uncovered the stunning data that a single white officer had participated in seven of the first nine fatal STRESS shootings during a five-month period. In the burst of publicity that followed, Peterson compared himself to a soldier in a war and attributed his frequent use of deadly force to the dangers of walking point in the undercover decoy operation.

In the spring of 1973, Patrolman Raymond Peterson was indicted for second-degree murder for the fatal shooting of Robert Hoyt, a 24-year-old African American male. He admitted to planting a knife on the victim's body but testified that his DPD superiors were really to blame for transforming an ordinary cop into a killer and celebrating his STRESS homicide ratio, which is the number of people he killed. A majority-white jury acquitted him despite overwhelming evidence. The circumstances of the Robert Hoyt incident necessarily cast doubt on the cover stories for all of Patrolman Peterson's previous shootings and also raise hard questions about systematic corruption in the DPD Homicide Bureau investigations and internal Trial Board proceedings that repeatedly cleared him, as well as the Wayne County Prosecutor's eight previous determinations of "justifiable homicide."

Any balanced historical assessment of Raymond Peterson's role in the STRESS operation must implicate broader DPD policies and the reflexive justification of deadly force by the Wayne County Prosecutor, not just the actions of an individual officer. The architects of STRESS—in particular Commissioner John

Nichols, Commander James Bannon, and Mayor Roman Gribbs—designed the operation to "effectively police the black community" through the omnipresent threat of deadly force and the empowerment of undercover units to exercise preemptive and discretionary violence on the streets. Patrolman Raymond Peterson was the deadliest individual officer in the deadliest police unit anywhere in the United States during the early 1970s, but he also did what he did as an instrument of the Detroit Police Department and the white political leadership of the city.

The Deadliest Police Officer in the Nation

Patrolman Raymond Peterson participated in eight fatal encounters in undercover decoy operations from April-November 1971 and personally shot and killed the African American male "suspects" in at least five of them, and probably seven. All of these incidents raise questions of excessive and unjustified force, and at least two appear likely to have been premeditated murder, a preview of Peterson's killing of the unarmed Robert Hoyt in March 1973.

Based on Peterson's admission that he planted a knife to frame Robert Hoyt, and the habit of many DPD officers to carry "drop" weapons in case they shot someone, the "discovery" of knives on the alleged suspects in many of these killings likely also involved a STRESS conspiracy to frame the victims. The Wayne County Prosecutor declared all eight of the fatal shootings that involved Raymond Peterson during 1971 to be "justifiable homicides." Each of these incidents is analyzed at length on the "Remembering STRESS Victims" page and summarized only briefly here. Excerpt from Michigan Civil Rights Commission investigation in late 1971 exposing Raymond Peterson's role.

Herbert Childress (May 11, 1971), a 35-year-old African American male, shot and killed by Patrolman Peterson acting as decoy inside a private apartment during a prostitution sting operation after Childress allegedly attacked the officer with a knife.

Clarence Manning, Jr. (May 29, 1971), a 25-year-old African American male, shot and killed by Patrolman Peterson acting as decoy backup from a distance of less than five inches away, contrary to his statement. In 1975, the city of Detroit settled a wrongful death lawsuit in recognition that a jury would find that the STRESS team used excessive force and lied about the encounter.

Horace Fennicks and Howard Moore (July 5, 1971), a 28-year-old African American male and a 32-year-old African American male, respectively, shot in the back and killed by Patrolman Peterson and another STRESS officer acting as decoy backup while both men fled the scene of an alleged mugging. The STRESS team "discovered" a knife on the victims. The city of Detroit later settled wrongful death lawsuits by both families.

James Smith (July 14, 1971), a 32-year-old African American male, shot and killed by Patrolman Peterson and other STRESS officers acting as decoy backup after allegedly being part of a group that tried to mug the decoy with a knife. The wounded survivors testified in the STRESS lawsuit that Smith was an innocent bystander and that the decoy team had initiated the attack and fabricated the entire encounter.

James Henderson (September 9, 1971), a 24-year-old African American male and eyewitness to Raymond Peterson's previous killing of Herbert Childress, shot and killed by Peterson and another STRESS officer inside a hotel after allegedly attacking them with a knife. The hotel clerk testified in the STRESS lawsuit that Peterson and his partner executed James Henderson in an act of premeditated murder.

Neil Bray (November 13, 1971), a 21-year-old African American male, shot and killed by Patrolman Peterson and other STRESS officers acting as decoy backup, after he allegedly attacked Peterson with a knife while fleeing from the decoy officer, who shot him from point-blank range in the chest in an act that the STRESS lawsuit labeled an "execution." [This story] burst back into the news in dramatic fashion after his fatal off-duty shooting of Robert Hoyt, a 24-year-old African American male. The anti-STRESS movement held three separate protests at DPD headquarters in the week after the incident, labeling him "Mad Dog Peterson" and demanding prosecution for murder. Before his coverup unraveled, Peterson told the *Detroit News* that he didn't "like taking another man's life, but it seems that I am a magnet for trouble."

"None of us believe the story those policemen told"—Robert Hoyt's brother to the *Michigan Chronicle*, before the DPD coverup of his murder unraveled.

There is indisputable evidence that Raymond Peterson fabricated his account of the Robert Hoyt incident and attempted to frame the deceased victim by planting a knife that the officer had brought to the scene of the crime. Forensic evidence proved that Peterson had been carrying the knife around in his pocket for at least a week, a clear illustration of the practice of many DPD officers to have "drop" weapons at the ready to justify an unjustified shooting. Peterson himself even admitted to making up the knife story as part of a risky but successful strategy as a trial defendant, after the Detroit Police Lab disproved his cover story and the Wayne County prosecutor charged him with second-degree murder.

Robert Hoyt Incident

The encounter began around 6:00 a.m. on March 9, 1973, when Robert Hoyt and Raymond Peterson allegedly were involved in a "sideswipe" car accident on the Fisher Freeway shortly after the officer had gone off duty and was driving home. Peterson, who was driving an unmarked car, claimed in his report that Hoyt caused the accident and then illegally fled the scene. Peterson and his off-duty partner, Patrolman Gary Prochorow, who was somehow (and suspiciously) also on the scene in a separate personal vehicle, then chased Robert

Hoyt down and shot at him several times from their moving vehicles. Raymond Peterson claimed that he finally managed to pull Robert Hoyt over but then had to shoot him dead because Hoyt first appeared to be reaching for a gun and then jumped out of the car and attacked the officer with a knife, slashing his jacket. Hoyt was actually unarmed, and after shooting him, Patrolman Peterson "discovered" a knife at the scene—just as he had in so many of his previous fatal shootings.

Patrolman Peterson's account of the Hoyt shooting was deeply suspicious even before the forensic evidence proved that he had planted the knife on the victim. Robert Hoyt's family and coworkers immediately denied that the 24-year-old, who had been on the way home from his job on the night shift at an automobile plant, could possibly have been carrying a knife. Relatives also accused the DPD investigation of covering up the evidence that his impounded car showed no signs of a "sideswipe," as Peterson claimed. His brothers also told the *Michigan Chronicle* that different STRESS units had continually harassed Robert Hoyt in the weeks before his death, which they speculated might have been because he was driving a used car that he had recently purchased from a known drug dealer. This raises the tantalizing possibility that what happened might not have been an off-duty police officer reacting with rage to a fender-bender but instead a targeted killing by a corrupt cop, perhaps even related to the extensive DPD complicity in the narcotics market and the Black community accusations of direct STRESS involvement (no specific evidence has emerged linking Peterson to narcotics corruption). Another possibility raised in the subsequent investigation was that Patrolman Peterson and Robert Hoyt might have been involved with the same African American woman and that the officer could have instigated the encounter for that reason. Several of Hoyt's friends told reporters that the two men had "hung out in the same bars" and previously argued over the woman, raising the possibility of a revenge hit by the off-duty officer that morning.

On March 22, the Wayne County Prosecutor charged Patrolman Peterson with second-degree murder after the Detroit Police Lab uncovered evidence that the knife that he claimed to have found on Robert Hoyt's body had cat hairs and fibers traceable to the officer's own pet and jacket pocket. The discovery was made by Mary Jarrett Jackson, an African American scientist in the DPD crime lab who went on to become the department's first female deputy chief. Prosecutor William Cahalan stated that Patrolman Peterson had shot Robert Hoyt in anger after the automobile worker accidentally rear-ended the officer's vehicle, and so the charge would be second-degree murder because the result was not premeditated. Cahalan declined to charge Peterson's partner, Gary Prochorow, even though the forensic evidence revealed that he had shot Robert Hoyt in the wrist during the car chase. The DPD removed both officers from the STRESS unit and suspended Peterson pending trial.

Trial and Acquittal

Raymond Peterson's second-degree murder trial
took place in early 1974, soon after the abolition
of STRESS by Coleman Young, Detroit's new
African American mayor. Peterson's counsel from
the DPOA union, Norman Lippitt, opened the
defense by admitting that his client had lied about
Robert Hoyt attacking him with a knife but insisted
that the officer had done so because "he actually
felt his life was in danger." The DPOA attorney
then took the extraordinary step of blaming
Peterson's actions on the higher-up officers
who designed STRESS and then "hid" in their
offices while tough patrolmen such as Raymond
Peterson "have to go out into the streets and deal
with robbers, muggers, pimps and prostitutes
while laying their lives on the line." Peterson
then testified that DPD commanding officers had
pressured the STRESS decoy squads to act more
aggressively after the first few quiet months of
early 1971 and then "congratulated us" whenever
they shot and killed suspects. During the cross-
examination, Peterson broke down crying when
confronted with the evidence of his fabrication of
Robert Hoyt's knife attack but insisted that he had
feared for his life on the side of the highway that
morning. Peterson said, through sobs: "Yes, I lied.
But I swear to God I'm telling the truth now"—
Raymond Peterson during cross-examination, Feb.
26, 1974.

Peterson's partner, Gary Prochorow,
also testified that Robert Hoyt had threatened
both of their lives by driving so recklessly that "I

actually thought the man was trying to kill us." Given that both officers were actually chasing Hoyt down the freeway at high speed, this witness testimony under oath seems like an obvious lie, designed to buttress the self-defense claim. In closing arguments, defense counsel Lippitt again blamed the DPD hierarchy for Hoyt's death, insisting that Raymond Peterson was "given a gun by an ignorant bureaucracy, and when he used it with fatal results, was lauded and praised by narrow-minded, non-thinking superiors." Peterson's attorney also blamed the criminality of Black Detroit for Peterson's actions in barely veiled racist language: "He was conditioned by the cruelty in the streets of this city, by the hate that permeated the very air we breathe."

In his instructions to the jury, Judge Joseph Maher arguably prejudiced the verdict by requiring them to evaluate Peterson's actions under the "reasonable discretion" standard for use of force by law enforcement officers, rather than the stricter standard for regular citizens, even though the policeman had been off duty and in his private car at the time of the incident. The judge told the jurors that in assessing Peterson's own state of mind, if he "reasonably believed that Robert Hoyt was about to do him great bodily harm, you are required to find the defendant not guilty." The jury, made up of 12 white members and 2 African Americans, then proceeded to acquit Raymond Peterson of second-degree murder.

"The miscarriage of justice that occurred in the recent murder case of Police Officer Raymond Peterson in Recorder's court tops all miscarriages of justice that have ever taken place in this country."—Thomas Bayliss in *Michigan Chronicle*, March 23, 1974.

African American residents of Detroit expressed outrage after Raymond Peterson's acquittal but also a profound sense of inevitability based on the traditional deference of white jurors toward police officers who killed Black citizens. The *Michigan Chronicle* reported at length on the anger and shock in the Black community and also emphasized that the defense counsel had disqualified many African Americans in order to obtain a mostly white jury pool of city residents predisposed to sympathize with the police. The *Chronicle* additionally ran commentary by enraged Black citizens such as Thomas Bayliss[...], who emphasized that Peterson had once again gotten away with murdering "a young Black man in cold blood." Bayliss dramatically labeled the verdict the greatest "miscarriage of justice" in the history of the United States.

Even Prosecutor William Cahalan, who had accepted with equanimity the acquittals of the police officers in the only other STRESS-related prosecution, the Rochester Incident trial, expressed dismay and confusion as to how "the jury could reach that verdict." And even the Detroit Police Department, which had almost always welcomed back officers who were charged with felonies but then acquitted, terminated Raymond Peterson after an internal Trial Board proceeding. The DPD's decision to punish a highly decorated STRESS officer after his ninth killing of an African American citizen was presumably based on Peterson's admission of lying in his incident report, but probably also not unrelated to his eagerness on the witness stand to blame commanding officers for his two-year killing spree.

"I really believed I was doing the right thing ... Whenever I shot someone, I would have to go to headquarters to fill out a report and the guys would cheer me when I walked in ... The brass in the department went out of its way to encourage me."—Raymond Peterson, Sept. 12, 1976.

In 1976, the *Detroit Free Press* published a lengthy profile of fired STRESS officer Raymond Peterson, shortly after he successfully took the Detroit Police Department to arbitration to receive two years of back pay and a disability pension. The article portrayed Peterson as a friendly middle-aged man, with the "eyes of a playful cat that suddenly purrs for affection." The working-class Detroit native was now working as a truck driver, but five years before he had been "a hero to the officials of the Detroit Police Department," an elite policeman and killer who "was doing exactly what he was conditioned and trained to do."

Looking back, two years after his acquittal for the murder of Robert Hoyt, Peterson reiterated his racist description of the Black neighborhoods of the city of Detroit as more dangerous than a jungle and their residents as more depraved than wild animals. "It's worse than a jungle on those streets," Peterson insisted, "because in a jungle the animals they just kill for food, but on those goddamn streets, boy, they will kill you just for kicks." Raymond Peterson then justified his own track record of deadly violence—he almost certainly killed more people than anyone else, whether police officer or civilian, in modern Detroit history—by drawing an ultimately murky distinction between the righteous side of the law versus the unwritten rules of the streets. "When the line comes down to push or shove and you got the hammer," the white man responsible for the deaths of nine African American men explained, "you got to use it because chances are you aren't going to get another chance."

Peterson then argued, rightly, that his superiors in the Detroit Police Department were also responsible for his actions, having designed and celebrated the lethality of the STRESS operation and repeatedly praised and rewarded him personally. "I really believed I was doing the right thing," the truck driver recalled. "We were cutting down on crime. They [the DPD hierarchy] were happy with me. Whenever I shot someone, I would have to go to headquarters to fill out a report and the guys would cheer me when I walked in … The brass in the department went out of its way to encourage me."

Although small in number, every police department in America has these types of police officers. These officers are the ones who abuse citizens, lack honesty, and have no integrity. They wreak havoc on city budgets by causing unnecessary lawsuits through their actions. These type of police officers are liars, selfish, arrogant, ignorant, self-entitled, abusive, controlling, hostile, frustrated, and sometimes dangerous. These types of officers make it difficult for reform-minded police chiefs to implement the necessary changes to improve their departments and provide better service to the community.

Lying must not be tolerated in any organization, especially in the police department and law enforcement. Truthfulness must be maintained and is essential in order for police departments to survive and function in an orderly manner. Citizens expect their police officers to possess the highest degree of honesty, integrity, and truthfulness. These traits are extremely important to preserve the public trust in law enforcement officers.

There is no place in law enforcement for bad officers who lie to exercise their personal agenda of protecting themselves in their wrongdoings.

6

BAD POLICING, BAD DECISIONS

Woe to those who call evil good, and good evil; Who substitute darkness for light and light for darkness; Who substitute bitter for sweet and sweet for bitter! (Isaiah 5:20)

WHILE WORKING AS AN EXECUTIVE officer in the Detroit Police Department, there were times when I was assigned to investigate the actions of police officers who were involved in shootings, fatalities, in-custody prisoner deaths, and other uses of force resulting in serious physical harm or death to police officers, suspects, or prisoners. In the Detroit Police Department, we called this type of investigation a Board of Review. The board consisted of three executive officers, with one executive holding a higher rank than the other two. The highest-ranking officer was assigned to chair this investigative board.

The purpose of the Board of Review was to evaluate all the

evidence in conjunction with the incident; review all relevant reports prepared; interview all relevant witnesses; determine whether or not any violations of department rules and regulations occurred; determine whether or not officers' actions were proper; identify and report any policy failures; and determine if any criminal laws had been violated. The board would then prepare a detailed report to be reviewed by other executives and the chief of police, who was responsible for the disposition of the case. My years of experience conducting police investigations allow me to objectively analyze and assess fatal incidents. In this chapter, I comment on recent cases of fatal force that were covered in the news media and video footage that was released to the public.

Tamir Rice

The following information was taken from a transcript by the International Commission of Inquiry on Systemic Racist Police Violence Against People of African Descent in the United States of America regarding the Tamir Rice Hearing, January 26, 2021.

> Tamir Rice was a boy of 12 years old who was playing in a park called the Cudell Recreation Center. In 2014, he was playing with a toy gun. A person in the park called 911. That person relayed to 911 that he was probably a juvenile and that it was probably a fake gun. The 911 dispatcher did not relay that information to the police officers. Two officers, Frank Garmback, and Timothy Loehmann arrived on the scene. First, they hopped the curb that led up to the park at Cudell recreation center, and they drove within feet of the gazebo under which Tamir was playing. Before the car came to a stop, as it was sliding on the grass,

jumped out of his car and within two seconds fired at Tamir. Timothy Loehmann who was essentially a rookie officer, had only been on the job for less than a year. Tamir's sister Tajai, who was playing at Cudell recreation center as well, ran to Tamir's aid. She was tackled to the ground and was prevented from giving any kind of comfort or medical aid to Tamir. The officers did not provide medical aid to Tamir.

The first person to provide medical aid was an FBI agent, who coincidentally, happened to be near the scene at that time. The officer who drove the vehicle, Frank Garmback had been with the Cleveland Police Department for a number of years, and received civil rights violations before that led to at least one civil rights lawsuit against him. However, no significant disciplinary actions were taken against him. Timothy Loehmann was an officer with the Independence police department. He was essentially forced to resign from that department before he even began his job. His training officer described him as emotionally unstable and incapable of handling a firearm. However, the Cleveland police department did not review the Independence police departments personnel files upon Timothy Loehmann's application to the Cleveland police department. Timothy Loehmann was approved for employment with the Cleveland police department in which he never should have been considered for employment.

One of the most important details is Timothy Loehmann claims that he ordered Tamir Rice three times to put his hands up. However, the video is clear that is a fictional interpretation of the events. The events happened so quickly it would have been impossible for three commands to have been ordered. Ms. Rice alluded to the windows being rolled up on the vehicle. There was simply no time for Tamir to react to any orders that were given and were incredulous as to whether any orders were given at all. The fact is Tamir was playing in a park and there was no danger to Tamir or to other kids in the park until those officers arrived. The officers created the danger and there was no emergency for the officers to respond to. The way in which they responded gave themselves no opportunity to resolve this peacefully.

The way Officer Garmback approached Tamir was a highly improper police maneuver. We hired a number of experts. A couple of them were former police officers, police chiefs, who described the way in which Frank Garmback's approach of Tamir was a highly improper police maneuver and it essentially created a danger for the rookie officer Timothy Loehmann. If they had simply stopped at an intersection, at a distance of 100 feet away and presented orders at that point, the situation would have de-escalated rather quickly. Timothy Loehmann should never have been hired. Frank Garmback had previous civil rights allegations against him. He was never disciplined in any serious way. Following the murder of Tamir Rice, the next phase of injustice begins. Timothy McGuinty, who was the chief prosecutor in Cuyahoga County at that time, presented the case against the officers to a grand jury. However, the way in which he presented the case, essentially sabotaged and undermined the case he was presenting and he intended to do so. He later stated he recommended to the grand jury that they not move forward with indicting the officers.

We were allowed to present two or three of our experts at the grand jury. Those experts described being treated in an incredibly hostile way by the prosecutors, including one of them, pointing a toy pistol at one of our experts. It was clear that the prosecution had absolutely no interest in actually creating any kind of criminal accountability. The officers were allowed at the grand jury to read written statements. This is an important detail from a legal standpoint, because they were allowed to prepare statements, and give them to the grand jury. However, the prosecutors did not cross examine the officers on the statements that they made. The officers could have taken the Fifth. However, they chose to give statements to the prosecutor because they have so much discretion, and the American legal system chose not to cross examine the officers even though the officers left themselves vulnerable to cross examination. We believe that the grand jury was also never informed that they could have asked cross examination questions of the officers. The Department of Justice more recently announced that their investigation had come to a conclusion with a finding that the officers not be charged. I believe that finding was announced in between Christmas and New Year's. McGuinty's announcement was also made in between Christmas and New Year, in a rather inconvenient time and at a time when people are more focused on family than the news.

The grand jury process was completely sabotaged and undermined by the prosecution. The internal administrative disciplinary process within the Cleveland police department, that was supposed to provide some measure of accountability, suspended Officer Garmback for a handful of days. Certainly, that was not the kind of punishment Ms. Rice and the Rice family has sought. He appealed that decision and they reduced it to something like two or three days. Timothy Loehmann was fired from his job. However, not because he murdered Tamir Rice. He was fired because he lied on his application. We met with the Department of Justice during the Obama administration. They were beginning their investigation and building the case. What we know now that before the most recent election in the United States, there was a whistleblower who came forward from within the Department of Justice. He said there are career prosecutors within the Department of Justice who wish to go forward with prosecuting these officers, with forming a grand jury to investigate and to potentially go forward with charges against the officers. However, what the whistleblower revealed is that political appointees made by the Trump administration appear to have sabotaged that attempt for the career prosecutors to go forward with a prosecution.

Career prosecutors in the Department of Justice twice recommended to their higher ups that they be allowed to move forward with forming a grand jury. And twice that request was essentially ignored for many months and over a year, and then finally denied. And to be clear, it is a routine thing to rubber stamp those requests when a career prosecutor has spent months and years building a case and building a file, and then makes a serious recommendation to move forward. This particularly when police officers are involved. It is unfortunate that in the United States, police officers for some reason ought not to be held to the same standards of legal and criminal accountability.

The Department of Justice did officially provide us with notification that they have come to a conclusion with their investigation, and that they have found that the officers did not violate the federal civil rights standards necessary to go forward. The other key part of that was the potential for obstruction of justice charges to be brought against the officers. Timothy Loehmann created a fictional account of the crime, that we believe he committed by essentially claiming that he ordered multiple times for Tamir to raise his hands. However, the video proves that that is simply an impossibility. He continued to repeat that lie even after it came to light that that video of the crime existed. The police union have very deep coffers, and they have protected the officers every step of the way. This is a tragedy that's been compounded at multiple levels of government.

My Perspective

After reviewing the videotape of the fatal shooting of Tamir Rice, I conclude that the shooting could have been avoided and that the responding officers were extremely negligent in how they responded to the scene. The callous way the officers conducted themselves was one of the worst displays of police work I have ever witnessed.

After receiving information from the dispatcher, the officers had the time and opportunity to plan a proper response. The way the officers approached Tamir Rice in their police car was highly improper. The officer driving the police vehicle positioned his vehicle less than ten feet from Tamir Rice. The improper positioning of the vehicle put both officers' lives in jeopardy. If Tamir had been a real criminal, both officers could have been shot and killed. What the officers should have done was to position their vehicle farther way to lessen the danger of being shot. This would have allowed the officers to use their vehicle as cover. This would also have given the officers an opportunity to communicate with Tamir Rice and warn him to put the gun down. The proper positioning of the vehicle could have prevented the use of fatal force by the officer against Tamir Rice. If they positioned their vehicle properly, it would have allowed Tamir Rice a chance to respond to the officers' commands (if any were given).

The extreme negligence of both officers placed Tamir Rice in a vulnerable position. At a minimum, the officer who shot Tamir Rice should have been charged, tried, convicted, and put in prison. Based upon the events as narrated in the International Commission of Inquiry on Systemic Racist Police Violence Against People of African Descent in the United States of America regarding the Tamir Rice Hearing, January 26, 2021, it appears that the criminal justice system on all levels—county, state, and federal—failed to bring justice to Tamir Rice and his family, which is shameful and troubling. The officer who shot and killed Tamir Rice should have been put in prison for his gross negligence. The Department of Justice under the Trump administration, not surprisingly, did nothing to bring justice to the family of Tamir Rice.

Terence Crutcher

The following information was taken from an abcnews.com. go.com article by Michael Edison Hayden entitled "What We Know about the Terence Crutcher Police Shooting in Tulsa, Oklahoma," published September 20, 2016. Hayden wrote:

> On September 16, 2016, dashcam video of the death of Terence Crutcher, an unarmed black man who authorities said was fatally shot by a police officer Friday night in Tulsa, Oklahoma, shows him with his hands in the air moments before the white officer fired her weapon. The officers who approached Crutcher, 40, were initially responding to what police described as a stalled vehicle. It was unknown to officers whether Crutcher was armed at that time, according to police. Betty Shelby, the white officer identified by police as the one who shot Crutcher, was not the only officer to draw a weapon on him, and any commands she received from her superiors before shooting Crutcher are unknown at this time.
>
> Officer Tyler Turnbough, who is also white, used a stun gun on Crutcher, according to police. The reason one officer drew a stun gun while another drew a handgun against the unarmed man remains unknown at this time, as does why he was considered a threat to officers in the first place. Tulsa police helicopter footage, perhaps the clearest of the videos released on Monday, shows Crutcher walking along the road at a measured pace with his hands in the air before being shot. The officers follow several feet behind him, and Crutcher does not stop or turn toward them until

he places his hands on top of his vehicle, a white SUV. First two, and then three officers form a line behind Crutcher.

In an audio recording from inside the helicopter, a voice speaks up and says, "Time for a Taser." "That looks like a bad dude too. Probably on something," says another voice. It remains unclear from the video what would have given that impression to the speaker. With three officers standing in a line behind Terence Crutcher and at least one more officer standing several feet behind them, the video shows, his body falls to the pavement. Blood pools around his body. Roughly two minutes appear to pass before anyone checks on him. Dashcam video also appears to show Crutcher's hands on top of the vehicle seconds before he was killed.

My Perspective

After reviewing the videotape of the fatal shooting of Terence Crutcher, I determined that the shooting could have been avoided and that the responding officers were grossly negligent in how they handled the incident. Terrance Crutcher was being investigated because his vehicle had stalled in the middle of the roadway. He did absolutely nothing that made him a threat to any of the officers. There were four officers at the scene prior to Crutcher being shot and an additional two officers flying above the scene in a police helicopter. There was no sense of urgency in this incident, and the officers had more than enough time to peacefully resolve the incident without using fatal force. At the time Crutcher was shot, both his hands were visible on the vehicle, and he was not acting aggressive. There is no evidence he was reaching for anything.

Police Officer Betty Shelby, who shot Crutcher, used the same tired historical police justification for the killing black people: "I feared for my life." There were three other police officers at the scene when Officer Shelby fired her weapon. One of the officers standing next to Officer Shelby unjustly fired his taser at Crutcher. It was not clear whether Officer Shelby fired her weapon before Crutcher was tased or after he was tased. Regardless, both officers were wrong for using any kind of force against Crutcher.

Two of the officers were standing immediately next to Officer Shelby. There were two other police officers flying above in a police helicopter. None of the other officers fired their weapons. Therefore, Crutcher could not have been a threat to anyone. He was a threat only in Officer Shelby's imagination. There was no reason for her to be scared. This was nothing but an execution by a cowardly officer unfit for police work. Although a jury found her not guilty, this cowardly officer should be occupying a prison cell for at least the next twenty years instead of walking around free. The Department of Justice under the Trump administration, not surprisingly, did nothing to bring justice to Crutcher's family.

Eric Garner

The following information was taken from an wikipedia.org news article entitled "Killing of Eric Garner":

> On July 17, 2014, Eric Garner was killed in the New York City borough of Staten Island after Daniel Pantaleo, a New York City Police Department (NYPD) officer, put him in a prohibited chokehold while arresting him. Video footage of the incident generated widespread national attention and raised questions about the appropriate use of force by law enforcement.

NYPD officers approached Garner on July 17 on suspicion of selling single cigarettes from packs without tax stamps. After Garner told the police that he was tired of being harassed and that he was not selling cigarettes, the officers attempted to arrest Garner. When Pantaleo placed his hands on Garner, Garner pulled his arms away. Pantaleo then placed his arm around Garner's neck and wrestled him to the ground. With multiple officers pinning him down, Garner repeated the words "I can't breathe" 11 times while lying face down on the sidewalk. After Garner lost consciousness, he remained lying on the sidewalk for seven minutes while the officers waited for an ambulance to arrive. Garner was pronounced dead at an area hospital approximately one hour later.

The medical examiner ruled Garner's death a homicide. According to the medical examiner's definition, a homicide is a death caused by the intentional actions of another person or persons. Specifically, an autopsy indicated that Garner's death resulted from "[compression] of neck, compression of chest and prone positioning during physical restraint by police". Asthma, heart disease, and obesity were cited as contributing factors.

On December 4, 2014, a Richmond County grand jury decided not to indict Pantaleo. This decision stirred public protests and rallies, with charges of police brutality made by protesters. By December 28, 2014, at least 50 demonstrations had been held nationwide in response to the Garner case, while hundreds of demonstrations against general police brutality counted Garner as a focal point. On July 13, 2015, an out-of-court settlement was reached, under which the City of New York would pay the Garner family $5.9 million. In 2019, the U.S. Department of Justice declined to bring criminal charges against Pantaleo under federal civil rights laws.

A New York Police Department disciplinary hearing regarding Pantaleo's treatment of Garner was held in the summer of 2019; on August 2, 2019, an administrative judge recommended that Pantaleo's employment be terminated. Pantaleo was fired on August 19, 2019, more than five years after Garner's death.

My Perspective

After reviewing the videotape of the fatal assault by police officers against Eric Garner, I have determined that his death could have been avoided and that the responding officers were grossly negligent in their handling of the incident. Selling loose cigarettes is not a felony, and the amount of force used against Eric Garner by the officers was deplorable, a violation of NYPD policy, and unnecessary. There were at least six officers at the scene. There was no reason for any officer to be scared or in fear of their life. At least four of the officers participated in restraining Garner. His pleas that he could not breathe were ignored and went unanswered by all of the involved officers, including Officer Pantaleo, whose arm was wrapped around Garner's neck. The type of force used on Garner was not consistent with his level of resistance. He was not a threat to any officer after he was taken to the ground and restrained by at least four police officers. After Garner lost consciousness, he remained lying on the sidewalk for seven minutes while the officers waited for an ambulance to arrive.

After the Richmond County grand jury decided not to indict

Officer Pantaleo, the Department of Justice should have intervened and brought charges against him. Again, justice has eluded another black citizen, killed for a minor offense, improperly handled by police. This type of bad policing must end if police departments are to regain the trust of the citizens they serve.

Philando Castile

The following information was taken from an wikipedia.org news article entitled "Killing of Philando Castile," which states:

> On July 6, 2016, Philando Castile, a 32-year-old African American man, was fatally shot during a traffic stop by police officer Jeronimo Yanez of the St. Anthony police department in the Minneapolis–Saint Paul metropolitan area.
>
> Castile was driving with his girlfriend, Diamond Reynolds, and her four-year-old daughter when at 9:00 p.m. he was pulled over by Yanez and another officer in Falcon Heights, a suburb of Saint Paul, Minnesota. After being asked for his license and registration, Castile told Officer Yanez that he had a firearm (Castile was licensed to carry) to which Yanez replied, "Don't reach for it then", and Castile said "I'm, I, I was reaching for ..." Yanez said "Don't pull it out", Castile replied "I'm not pulling it out", and Reynolds said "He's not ..." Yanez repeated "Don't pull it out". Yanez then fired seven close-range shots at Castile, hitting him five times. Castile died of his wounds at 9:37 p.m. at Hennepin County Medical Center, about 20 minutes after being shot.

Reynolds posted a live stream video on Facebook in the immediate aftermath of the shooting, and the incident quickly gained international interest. Local and national protests formed, and five months after the incident, Yanez was charged with second-degree manslaughter and two counts of dangerous discharge of a firearm. After five days of deliberation, he was acquitted of all charges in a jury trial on June 16, 2017. After the verdict, Yanez was immediately fired by the City of Saint Anthony. Wrongful death lawsuits against the city brought by Reynolds and Castile's family were settled for a total of $3.8 million.

My Perspective

After reviewing the videotape of the fatal shooting of Philando Castile, I determined the shooting could have been avoided. Further, the responding officers were grossly negligent in their handling of the incident.

This was one of the worst incidents that I have seen mishandled by the police. Officer Yanez had multiple options he could have used to handle this unfortunate incident. The officers stopped Castile for a traffic offense. There is no way that this should have escalated into a police execution. Castile clearly advised the officer that he was armed. In most states, citizens who have a permit to carry a weapon must advise police officers that they are armed. This was the point where Officer Yanez should have used the proper commands to make the situation safe. (1) Officer Yanez could have advised Castile that he would return to his scout car and that he (Castile) could look for the paperwork requested and place it on the dashboard so that he (Yanez) could see it, and then place his hands visibly on the steering wheel.

(2) Officer Yanez could have ordered Castile's girlfriend out the car, had him place his weapon on the passenger front seat, and then have Castile exit the vehicle, and his partner could have retrieved the gun from the front seat. This was awful police work, but the jury rewarded the officer with a not-guilty verdict. This officer participated in an execution of an innocent citizen and should be in prison.

Daunte Wright

The following information was taken from a wikipedia.org news article entitled "Killing of Daunte Wright":

> On April 11, 2021, Daunte Wright, a 20-year-old biracial Black man, was fatally shot by police officer Kimberly Potter during a traffic stop and attempted arrest for an outstanding arrest warrant in Brooklyn Center, Minnesota. Wright was driving with his girlfriend in his white 2011 Buick Lacrosse. At 1:53 p.m. local time on April 11, 2021, Brooklyn Center police pulled them over on 63rd Avenue North; officers said that they did so due to the car's expired registration tag/ sticker on license plate. According to prosecutor Pete Orput, they later noticed the presence of an air freshener hanging from the car's rearview mirror, in violation of Minnesota law. Officers ran Wright's name through a police database and learned that he had an open arrest warrant after failing to appear in court on charges that he fled from officers and possessed a gun without a permit during an encounter with Minneapolis police in

June. Based on that information, police attempted to arrest him.

Police body camera footage showed two male officers and one female officer (Potter) approaching the car. One officer approached the driver's side door. The other officer approached the passenger's side door, while Potter, who was acting as a training officer, stood back initially.

The first officer informed Wright that there was a warrant for his arrest. He opened the driver's side door and Wright stepped out of the car. The car door remained open while Wright put his hands behind his back and the officer attempted to put on handcuffs. After several moments, Potter approached the pair. She held a vehicle's proof of insurance card with her right hand, then moved it to her left hand.

Wright, who was unarmed, began trying to avoid arrest, struggled with the officers, broke free, and stepped back into his car. Potter, who when the incident started had her Taser holstered on her left side and her gun on her right, said, "I'll tase you," and then yelled, "Taser! Taser! Taser!" Instead of a Taser, Potter then discharged her firearm a single time using her right hand, and subsequently said, "Oh shit, I just shot him."

Potter's pistol, a Glock 9 mm model, was black, metal and almost a pound heavier than her plastic Taser, described as yellow or neon-colored, with a black grip. Potter was holding her gun for at least seven seconds before discharging it. Immediately after shooting Wright, she was still holding the proof-of-insurance card with her left hand.

My Perspective

After reviewing the videotape of the fatal shooting of Daunte Wright, I determined the shooting could have been avoided and the responding officers were grossly negligent in their handling of the incident. Wright was stopped for a minor traffic offense. Black citizens should not be shot by white officers for minor traffic offenses. There were two additional officers at the scene, and neither of those officers felt the need to fire their weapon.

Officer Potter's actions were reckless, careless, and against department guidelines. Officer Potter had no legitimate reason to pull her weapon under these circumstances, because Daunte Wright was seated in his car, struggling with another officer. She had more than enough time to assess if Wright was a legitimate threat to any officer. She should go to prison for her reckless actions.

Policing is a very difficult and dangerous job. I am well aware of the dangers of police work because of my thirty-three-plus years of service. During my career, I have been involved in some of the most dangerous and intense situations a police officer can be involved in. However, I have never shot anyone, and I've never been accused of using excessive force.

I wrote this chapter to expose serious problems with the decision-making about fatal force being used by white police officers against black people. There is a disparity in treatment when some white police officers interact with black citizens. As a police officer myself, I have experienced the disparaging treatment from white police officers even after I identified myself as police officer. A white Michigan State Trooper wrote me a ticket while I was on duty responding to a homicide scene, driving my unmarked department police vehicle. Another time, a white Michigan State Trooper prepared a false felony police report against me and attempted to get a warrant issued. If they treat a black police executive officer in this manner, how do you think they are treating black citizens they encounter? Ninety-nine percent of the time when I've been stopped by white officers, they have been respectful and courteous. It is the 1 percent of officers who are destroying the reputation of police departments nationwide, white officers with their hatred, racism, and bad decision-making.

I strongly believe that transparency must be unceasing in all instances where police officers use force when investigating or apprehending suspects. This transparency must be followed up with accountability, discipline, and, when necessary, incarceration. The incidents written about in this chapter clearly reveal there are failures in law enforcement. These failures include prosecutors failing to charge police officers when they use excessive force; police chiefs failing to provide leadership and holding police officers accountable; police unions that blindly support their members when their actions are blatantly wrong; grand juries failing to indict police officers for their wrongdoing; and failures of the Department of Justice, which allows politics to influence whether officers are investigated or charged. America cannot afford to be lax in its response to these failures. Police reform must become more than a pacifier. It has to be meaningful and effective in reality.

The entire criminal justice system must be repaired. If not, then America will continue to decline and wallow in public protests, demonstrations, riots, civil unrest, and a public with no faith in its criminal justice system.

7

THE COST OF POLICE SILENCE

Have nothing to do with the fruitless deeds of darkness, but rather expose them. (Ephesians 5:11)

ONE OF THE MAIN ISSUES that must be corrected by police departments nationwide is when colleagues remain silent when fellow officers commit misconduct. This silence is destroying the faith and confidence of the citizens they serve. There is no valid reason that officers should conceal the actions of police misconduct they've witnessed. The failure to report all incidents of police misconduct by peers compromises the integrity, honesty, and trust of all police departments in the communities they serve. This silence destroys the faith, confidence, and morale of those officers who do not support the wrongful actions perpetrated by their peers.

This silence causes stress in the work environment and is detrimental how police departments function and operate. Deferring to silence in not reporting police misconduct not only permeates the police officer ranks, it can permeate through first line supervisors and upward. Some supervisors have close relationships with the officers they supervise, and depending on the misconduct or violation, they may turn their eyes away from holding officers accountable. Many first line supervisors feel the need to protect officers because they have off-duty friendships with them, as well as on-duty relationships with them.

I have worked in both large and small police departments. During my twenty-nine years of service in the Detroit Police Department, it was an unwritten policy that officers promoted to the ranks of lieutenant and sergeant should not be returned to their previous assignment. This ensured that newly promoted officers would not supervise officers they previously worked with. This was a great policy for newly promoted officers and the department. It prevented newly promoted officers from showing allegiance to the people they formerly worked with. This prevents claims of favoritism by other officers and makes for a more positive work environment.

In a smaller police department, it is not possible to institute this policy because of its size. Therefore, the silence in smaller departments is magnified more because it is likely that supervision and officers worked more closely together and more regularly than in larger departments. They have closer relationships and more than likely worked together as peers. This sometimes create an atmosphere of allegiance, compromise, and reluctance for accountability to discipline when misconduct is revealed or discovered. Supervisors seldom seek to expose or discipline a former partner of misconduct. Supervisors and officers use Acute Justification Syndrome (AJS) to justify misconduct and violations of department rules, regulations, and department policy, as well as violations of the law. I must clearly state that this is not normal in most police departments. However, this type of conduct does occur on occasions in nearly every police department in America, but it should never be accepted or embraced. The public trust must always be considered first, and the reputation of the police department should not be tarnished.

When officers are silent, it causes major damage to police departments in cities across the nation. In order to combat the high cost of officer silence, we must look at why officers stay silent when their colleagues commit improprieties. We must closely monitor and explore the cost of being silent by officers who witness misconduct by their peers.

Officers who remain silent indirectly support the bad actions of their fellow officers. Silent police officers are the reason why some officers accumulate numerous complaints and lawsuits over the course of their careers. This silence prevents supervisors and management from identifying problem officers and denies management the opportunity to correct this negative behavior. History reveals that if problem officers go unchecked, they more than likely will commit major offenses that lead to severe injury or death in the future.

In the George Floyd murder case, police officer Derek Chauvin amassed about eighteen complaints during his career. None of those complaints resulted in disciplinary action. As a result of this nonaction, Officer Chauvin murdered George Floyd by choking him to death, placing his knee on his neck while handcuffed lying on the ground. Chauvin was subsequently charged with murder and was found guilty by a jury. The family of George Floyd was awarded $27 million. Additionally, Officer Chauvin's actions against George Floyd resulted in hundreds of millions of dollars of damages to businesses nationwide as a result of his deplorable conduct.

In the city of Detroit, police officers Larry Nevers and Walter Budzyn both accumulated significant numbers of complaints during their careers. It was reported that Officer Nevers accumulated twenty-five complaints during his career, and Officer Budzyn accumulated nineteen complaints. As a result of this inaction, Nevers and Budzyn murdered unarmed Malice Green by beating him to death with a steel flashlight. They both were convicted of second-degree murder. It was reported that Larry Nevers had four lawsuits involving excessive force claims against him. In 1973, the city of Detroit paid a settlement of $275,000 for claims of excessive force by Nevers. Nevers cost the city of Detroit another use of force settlement over $5 million for the murder of Malice Green.

On January 28, 2015, in the city of Inkster, Michigan, police officer William "Robocop" Melendez was seen on video footage from his car's camera assaulting Floyd Dent, an unarmed citizen. It was reported that Officer Melendez struck Floyd Dent sixteen times in the face while placing him in a chokehold. Dent was also tased multiple times by other police officers and kicked while lying on the ground. Dent suffered numerous injuries from Officer Melendez's assault, including a broken orbital socket in one of his eyes. Officer Melendez was charged with and convicted of assault and sentenced to thirteen months to ten years in prison. During the Floyd Dent incident, Officer Melendez had a pending lawsuit against him for excessive force. He was accused of beating a suspect so badly, the suspect defecated on himself. The incident occurred in July 2014.

Prior to working in the Inkster Police Department, Officer Melendez worked in the Detroit Police Department and had a significant history of complaints of use of force; therefore, the name "Robocop" was given to him by people who knew him in Detroit. In 2003, more than a dozen officers were indicted on criminal charges for allegedly stealing drugs, guns, and money from suspected drug dealers, as well as planting evidence and falsifying reports. Melendez was accused of being the ringleader. He was acquitted at trial in 2004 and resigned from the Detroit Police Department in 2007. Officer Melendez had numerous complaints against him while working for the Detroit Police Department. He was named in twelve lawsuits, one lawsuit costing the City of Detroit over $1 million. The Floyd Dent lawsuit cost the city of Inkster over $1 million. Property taxes had to be increased and assessed to the residents to pay for the lawsuit.

There is a clear correlation between officers with numerous complaints and future escalations into more serious crimes or fatal assaults. This stone-cold silence in police departments has cost cities and municipalities across the United States hundreds of millions of dollars in lawsuits. This silence has indirectly cost hundreds of millions of dollars in property damage to businesses across America during civil disturbances and riots because of the actions and conduct of tainted police officers. This culture of silence must stop now.

However, there is a tremendous cost to honest police officers who step forward and report improper conduct by tainted colleagues. Honest police officers have to endure many unpleasant things if they are found to be exposing improper conduct by their peers. Honest police officers will have to endure being ostracized, ridiculed, alienated, and isolated; they may even face reprisals from their peers. This reprisal comes in the form of not receiving backup on their police runs, being labeled a "snitch," failure to provide information on dangerous suspects, damaging an officer's personal vehicle, hiding their department-issued police equipment, and veiled threats to an officer's family or loved ones.

In order to address the problem of silence in police departments, police chiefs, city managers, mayors, and other politicians must understand the temperament and psyche of those officers who believe it's okay to intimidate their colleagues who are seeking to do things the right way. These officers, usually described as having a Type A personality, must be identified and their conduct must be closely monitored by first line supervisors and commanding officers. If not identified, they can easily influence passive peers into following something that is detrimental to the department's operations and damages the public trust to the citizens we swore to protect and serve. Police chiefs, city managers, and mayors must be aware of the tactics used by Type A officers, especially in smaller police departments. Type A officers will try to take away the power of reformed-minded police chiefs, by manipulating the unions, media, press, and other means to exercise their personal agenda to gain power.

Before I go any further, I must make known that I am not a trained psychologist or psychiatrist. I'm characterizing what I call Type A police officers based on my personal interactions with police officers during my thirty-three years in law enforcement. This chapter is just my personal and professional opinion of officers based upon previous conduct observed and heard.

Type A police officers exhibit certain traits and emotions during certain situations and activities. These officers have certain needs and desires that are reflective in their personalities and actions. Type A police officers influence and control other officers based upon the strength of their personality traits and conduct. They possess most (if not all) of the traits described below. These Type A officers cause most of the problems in police departments across the country.

1. **Dominant/Controlling.** Type A police officers are among the most vocal in the police department. They enjoy the influence and perceived respect and admiration they have over their peers. Type A officers usually have a position in the police union; they believe they can control the direction of the police department and regularly challenge the police chief, using their position in the union to achieve their personal agenda. These officers are found in every police department in the country but are more magnified in smaller police agencies. Type A police officers, regardless of their rank, education, or lack of management training, believe they are more qualified and more intelligent than the police chief and allow their arrogance and ignorance to get in the way of sound judgment and decision-making. Type A police officers usually have an extensive disciplinary

history and a long record of citizen's complaints filed against them. Type A officers are unreasonable in their thought process; when they don't get their way, they tell lies about the police chief.

2. **Aggressive.** Type A police officers are almost always aggressive when dealing with the public. They are usually at the top for arrests, but their tactics and use of force are questionable. They are usually at or near the top in citizen's complaints and lawsuits. They have lower seniority and feel the need to prove themselves. They are easily influenced by senior officers and have a difficult time going against them. They make many mistakes and depend on the experience of senior officers to cover for these mistakes.

3. **Hostile/Frustrated.** Type A police officers usually have high seniority and are frustrated and even hostile regarding the way their career path has taken them. They are difficult toward supervisors and upper management. They can be disruptive and are often unhappy and will take out their frustrations on the public. They are frustrated because of lack of recognition within the department, and they are usually underperformers and underachievers. They constantly complain about the decisions of upper management and believe they are better suited to run the police department. They are resistant to change, even though the change is for the betterment of the department. They possess the other traits mentioned but are not as aggressive or dominant because of their frustration.

4. **Entitled.** Type A police officers have an extreme sense of entitlement. Officers with this sense of entitlement can be the most dangerous type of officer in police departments nationwide. They believe they are entitled to any and all privileges, because they risk their lives protecting and serving the public. These officers believe that nothing is off limits to them. When they make mistakes, whether

intentional or unintentional, they should not be held accountable. They believe that justification should be made in all their wrongdoings. Type A police officers usually have high incidents of use of force, as well as high incidents of citizen complaints. They have an overly inflated ego and are much more ignorant and arrogant than they realize. They never take responsibility for their shortcomings, and every problem is always someone else's fault.

These are the types of tainted police officers that the good, honest, integrity-filled officers must deal with if they report incidents of misconduct. Although low in numbers, these tainted officers use intimidation tactics to maintain the blue wall of silence in police departments nationwide. These hostility tactics protect racists, white supremacists, and all other bottom-feeders who are masquerading as police officers and deceiving the public. They cloak themselves in honor and integrity, but their actions and conduct differ. Their conduct is destructive to law enforcement and is harmful to the trust of the people they swore to protect and serve. They need to turn in their badge and gun, and find something else to do.

As a rookie police officer in the Detroit Police Department, I experienced firsthand what tainted officers will do if you don't agree with their arrest tactics. It was July in 1978. I was walking a beat with my partner in our designated area and monitoring my police radio. It was in the middle of July, and the weather was nice and warm. I was working the afternoon shift with my partner. We had made all of our rounds, checking the businesses in our area to make sure they were secure. We were anxious to get into some real action.

Just before sundown, a radio transmission came over my radio. It was the scout car in our area, announcing they were chasing someone in a stolen blue Chevy. Me and my partner started monitoring the radio closely. We were hoping that we would see some real police action. We continued to monitor the radio closely, and lo and behold, the scout car and chase started getting closer and closer to our assigned area. The scout car announced that the stolen car was traveling eastbound, directly on the street we were walking on. About five hundred feet to the west of us, we observed the suspect jump out of the stolen blue Chevy and run north between the houses. We started running at full speed in the direction where the suspect ran between the houses. My partner ran in one direction, and I ran in the other direction. A radio transmission from the scout car officer stated that the suspect was jumping the fences in the back yard. I ran into the back yard nearest to me and saw the suspect jumping fences, coming directly toward me. The suspect was approximately one hundred and fifty feet in front of me. I then observed one of the scout car partners tackle the suspect to the ground.

At this time, I had arrived at the backyard where the suspect was tackled. The scout car officer had handcuffed the suspect, and the suspect was not resisting. His partner had not made it to the scene yet. Shortly, his partner arrived at the scene. His partner drew his foot back to kick the suspect as he was lying on the ground, handcuffed.

When I observed this, I instinctively blurted out, "Stop, I will tell."

The officer stopped the forward motion of his leg and stared directly at me. He stated, "Rookie, you don't have enough time on the job to tell jack-shit."

I said to him, "If you want to, we can discuss this at Internal Affairs in the morning."

He glared back at me and stated, "Oh, you must be one of them."

I said, "Whatever one of them is, that's exactly who I am."

He and his partner helped the suspect up from the ground. He turned and stared me down with a menacing look, again, and then walked the suspect to his scout car and placed him under arrest.

As they were conveying the suspect to the car, my partner showed up and was upset that he was not able to get in on the action. He asked what happened, and I told him, "Nothing much. Just a routine arrest for a stolen car." We returned to our assigned beat and continued working our area until it was time to get off-duty.

When it was time to get off-duty, the scout car patrolling our area was supposed to pick us up and drive us to the police station for off-duty roll call. Well, you guessed it. The officers who arrested the person in the stolen Chevy, the officer I was going to tell on if he kicked the suspect, were responsible for transporting us back to the station. When we called for them to pick us up, all we could hear was static in the background. We requested the dispatcher to try to contact them, but they did not answer. The dispatcher advised us to start walking to the station, and he would try to find a ride for us. Needless to say, the ride never came. While walking back to the station, the scout car officers responsible for picking us up saw us and mockingly stated, "Rookies, do you want a ride?" Me and my partner started walking toward the car. As we got closer, the officers laughed at us, called us suckers, and pulled off quickly. My partner asked me what that was all about. While walking back to the station, I told my partner what had occurred at the scene of the arrest.

All my partner could say was, "Wow."

During my conversation with my partner, I told him, "I will not go to jail for anybody."

We walked nearly four miles back to the station and did not get back until 12:45 a.m. I was livid. The lieutenant advised me to calm down and said he was putting us in for overtime. I was not concerned about the overtime, but the disrespectful callous way we were treated.

From that day forward, and for the rest of my career, whenever I got a new partner, I would make it perfectly clear that "I will not go to jail for anybody." I did not care whether they liked me or not; I was not going to jail covering up what some tainted officer had done while working with me. This attitude did have repercussions. Shortly after the incident, the white officers quit speaking to me and would not be anywhere near me. I was isolated, alienated, ostracized, and ridiculed. However, that did not bother me as long as they did not try to put their hands on me. They scratched my car up a couple of times, but that stopped when I purchased an old ragged used car to drive to work.

Shortly after the stolen vehicle incident, I was reassigned off my beat to a scout car. The supervisor had to split up the senior officers, because there were too many unconfirmed rookies working, and unconfirmed rookies could not work a scout car together. The officer I was assigned to work with was not happy that he was assigned to work with me. After all, the incident regarding my actions had gotten around, and the white senior police officers did not want to work with me. After roll call, I went to our assigned scout car and got into the vehicle passenger side. My partner got inside the car and stated, "You can't drive the scout car; don't touch nothing, not the radio, run sheet, microphone. I mean don't touch nothing."

I looked at him and said, "Okay." As my partner drove the car from the station, a chilled silence was hovering inside the scout car.

After traveling about a quarter-mile from the station, I said to my partner, "I need to ask you something so that I'm perfectly clear on what you require of me."

My partner replied, "Go ahead."

I said, "You told me not to touch nothing; is that correct?" My partner stated yes.

I then asked him, "If you are getting your ass kicked by the homeboys, do you want me to touch them to get them up off of you?"

My partner gave me a menacing look while turning two shades of red, turned the scout car around, went back to the station, and went home sick.

When you are labeled a snitch by tainted, unworthy, flawed police officers, these are some of the things you have to go through while standing steadfast with honesty and integrity. Nothing I went through was as serious as what New York City Detective Frank Serpico went through, as written in *Frank Serpico Biography* in Americans Who Tell the Truth.Org.

"Frank Serpico's career as a plainclothes police detective working in Brooklyn and the Bronx to expose vice racketeering was short-lived, however, because he swam against the tide of corruption that engulfed the New York City police department during the late sixties and early seventies. Not only did he consistently refuse to take bribes for 'looking the other way,' he risked his own safety to expose those who did. In 1967 he reported to appropriate officials 'credible evidence of widespread, systemic police corruption.' It was not until April 1970, however, when the *New York Times* published an explosive story, that Mayor Lindsay took action and appointed the Knapp Commission to investigate. As a consequence of his testimony before the commission, Frank Serpico was ostracized by his peers and, many believe, ultimately 'set up' to be shot during a drug raid in which he was seriously wounded and his fellow officers did not call for assistance.

"Frank Serpico resigned from the New York City police department and spent the next ten years living abroad, recovering from his wounds, traveling and learning. In the early eighties he settled in New York State. His police career has been well documented in Peter Maas's best-selling biography and in the Academy Award nominated film, *Serpico*, in which Al Pacino portrayed him."

Officers who report misconduct must have the unbridled support of the police chief. Police chiefs must ensure that the officer is not working in a hostile environment. Police chiefs must develop clear and precise written rules, regulations, and directives that ensure that officers who denigrate another officer because of reporting misconduct will be disciplined. This will go a long way toward breaking the blue wall of silence that permeates many police departments.

8

DIVINE SPIRITUAL GUIDANCE

My help comes from the LORD, who made heaven and earth. (Psalm 121:2)

I BELIEVE THE MOST EFFECTIVE thing police officers can possess while discharging their duties as law enforcement officers is divine spiritual guidance. The foundation for the creation of nearly all of the laws that exist today is found in God's divine words, the holy Bible. In order to understand divine spiritual guidance and discernment, police officers need to read and study the Bible. Divine spiritual guidance is utilizing related Bible scriptures and applying them to all your duties and responsibilities as a police officer. Later in this chapter, I will provide Bible scriptures that I believe, if applied correctly, will greatly assist police officers when discharging their duties.

Police officers need to possess spiritual discernment in order to effectively discharge their duties. Spiritual discernment is a gift from God almighty that makes known something that cannot be perceived by natural means. It allows you to be able to distinguish, discern, judge, or appraise a person, statement, or situation.

In order to receive divine spiritual guidance and discernment, you must believe in God the Creator, believe that Jesus is the Son of God, believe that Jesus died on the cross to pay for the sins of the entire world, confess that you are a sinner and ask for forgiveness, and be baptized so that you may receive the Holy Spirit. The Holy Spirit is the channel through which you receive divine spiritual guidance and discernment, which allows you to be able to distinguish, discern, judge, or appraise a person, statement, or situation. In order to activate divine spiritual guidance and discernment, you must humble yourself and seek God the Creator through prayer. Prayer is the channel that allows you to speak with God and express your desires or concerns. In return, God will speak to you through the Holy Spirit within you, which in turn will provide divine spiritual guidance and discernment, which will allow you to rightly distinguish, discern, judge, or appraise a person, statement, or situation. However, divine spiritual guidance and discernment will not be given or received, if things are in conflict with the will of God. The Bible teaches us that God's ways are not our ways, and his thoughts are not our thoughts.

God's holy word teaches us that we have two spirits fighting within us. The good spirit fights with the bad spirit. Whenever we have the desire to do good, evil is present. Understanding and seeking divine spiritual guidance and discernment while discharging your policing duties can lead officers to great success in solving crimes, making the right decisions, treating people fairly (including suspects and prisoners), and discharging their duties.

As a Christian and believer in God's holy word, I have sought divine spiritual guidance and discernment in my personal life, as well as at various times over the course of my law enforcement career. Seeking divine spiritual guidance and discernment has been at the forefront during my career in law enforcement. The following stories will show you how divine spiritual guidance and discernment has worked in my police career, as well as my personal life.

While working in the Detroit Police Department as the commanding officer of the Carjacking Task Force, I utilized divine spiritual guidance on many occasions and in nearly every situation regarding the operations of the task force. Whether it be personnel decisions, disciplinary decisions, deployment of personnel, or operations, I utilized divine spiritual guidance.

The Carjacking Task Force was a multijurisdictional plainclothes task force consisting of Detroit Police, Wayne County Sheriff, Macomb County Sheriff, Michigan State Police, and Warren Police. The majority of the police officers on the task force were Detroit Police officers. There were twenty-two officers assigned to the task force, including myself. The task force was charged with investigating carjackings in Wayne, Oakland, and Macomb Counties; 95 percent of the carjackings at that time were occurring in the city of Detroit. During the previous year, before I took command of the task force, Detroit was averaging 388 carjackings per month and nearly forty-eight hundred reported cases per year. Needless to say, my task was daunting, considering I had to investigate carjackings in three counties with only twenty-two police officers. However, I knew that I had divine spiritual guidance and discernment at my disposal, and I could utilize it anytime I needed it.

One Wednesday afternoon, I was in my office reviewing all the paperwork involving the arrest of five carjacking suspects involved in a carjacking ring on the far east side of Detroit. My officers were putting the finishing touches on their paperwork after working all night. These suspects were wreaking havoc on the east side. We were able to connect them to seven carjackings. My officers got confessions from four of the suspects, and we were able to recover a significant amount of evidence relating to all five carjackings.

While reviewing paperwork related to the case, I got a call from the chief's office, saying he wanted to see me. I knew right away from previous phone calls from the chief's office that he had something important he wanted me to investigate. I could tell how important the chief's issue was by the rank he would address me by (I was a lieutenant on the task force). Depending on the importance of the chief's issue, he would jokingly address me in a rank one or two ranks lower than my rank of lieutenant.

True to form, when I entered the chief's office, he said, "Police Officer Napoleon, I heard the crooks were having a good time up on 7 Mile Road, even carjacking off-duty police officers; what are you going to do about this?"

I advised the chief that I would mobilize the entire carjacking task force on Friday night and jokingly told him we would have someone arrested and in custody by Saturday morning.

The chief said, "Great, make sure you call me Saturday morning."

I then left the chief's office and returned to my office.

Once I returned to my office, I looked up at the offense map and observed all the carjackings that had occurred on 7 Mile Road. It looked like hundreds of carjackings had occurred. Mind you, 7 Mile Road is one of the longest running streets in the city of Detroit. It runs from the far western border to the far eastern border of the city. To get a better understanding of how large an area the city of Detroit is, you can put the cities of San Francisco, Cleveland, and Boston inside the city limits of Detroit. One of our largest police precincts is bigger than those cities. The city of Detroit is 142 square miles.

After looking at the offense map, I began to feel the pressure and the magnitude regarding the task in front of me. I began to regret telling the chief I would have someone in custody by Saturday morning, even though I was only joking.

I began to reflect on the other times the police chief called me into his office about other carjacking cases. I realized that this was only the fifth time the chief called me into his office, even though we were getting hundreds of cases each month. I began to reflect on those other cases. The other four times the chief called me into his office, we discussed the following carjacking cases: (1) When two suspects went on a carjacking spree, carjacking a doctor in a prominent Detroit neighborhood and raping a female citizen in her car in front of her two infant children, fleeing to Toledo, Ohio, and committing a home invasion and carjacking in Toledo; returning to Michigan and committing four carjackings in four downriver communities. (2) The rape and carjacking of a female corrections officer. (3) The carjacking, robbery, and fatal shooting of a female citizen. (4) The carjacking and robbery of a Detroit Police lieutenant.

I remembered jokingly telling the chief in each of the previous four cases, that the Carjacking Task Force would have a suspect in custody the next day. Other than my foolish declarations of having suspects in custody the next day, I began to reflect on what other things those four cases had in common. After a few minutes of deep contemplation, I remembered closing the door to my office and in each of those cases praying to God and asking for divine spiritual guidance and discernment. I also remembered that the Carjacking Task Force solved all four cases. In each of the four cases, we had suspects in custody the next day. I must note that until I mentioned it in this book, I've never discussed with any of my officers about praying regarding any of our carjacking cases. I did not want to impose my personal religious beliefs on anyone working under me in a work environment. After reflecting on the four cases and the success we had arresting suspects in each case, the pressure and the magnitude regarding our task in front of us began to ease.

I must note that I never told any of my officers about my foolish declarations I made to the police chief, regarding having suspects in custody the next day. I did not want to put any unnecessary pressure on them. It was hard enough to investigate and solve carjackings, and I would be wrong to put unrealistic expectations on my officers.

I began to feel grateful and thankful to God for sending me his divine spiritual guidance in helping me solve those four very important cases. Being at ease now, I began to focus on the things I needed to do in order to be successful on Friday night. Looking at the carjacking offense map, I knew in advance that it would be impossible to cover East and West 7 Mile Road with just twenty-two police officers. I knew that the most important decision for me to consider would be to select the best area on 7 Mile Road to deploy the task force. Splitting up the task force would not be effective. East and West 7 Mile Road was very similar in many ways. They both consisted of mostly businesses with very few residential areas. The type of businesses on East and West 7 Mile were similar, consisting of banks, party stores, gas stations, restaurants, bakeries, fast food restaurants, bars, rental halls, barber shops, beauty shops, and nightclubs.

After staring at the offense map for minutes, I began to feel tired and sleepy. I had been up all night with the task force, directing them in the case we just closed. None of the members of the task force went home, because we had multiple suspects to process and fingerprint, and reports to be completed and warrants typed. We worked all through the night and most of the following day. I queried the sergeants on the progress of the paperwork. Because the officers made substantial progress, I dismissed them for the rest of the day. I knew we would have a long night on Friday and wanted my officers to be as fresh as possible.

On Friday, I went into the office early to prepare for the upcoming shift. There were a few officers who arrived early. My officers seem to like it when the entire task force is mobilized. They realize the seriousness of the task at hand and seem to look forward to the challenge.

While sitting in my office, I looked up at the offense map focusing on 7 Mile Road. I realized that I had to make a decision soon as to where to deploy the task force. I got up from my desk, closed the door to my office, and returned to my desk. I bowed my head and started to pray to God the Creator. I asked him to place me and the Carjacking Task Force in the right place tonight to be successful. I continued to stare at the carjacking offense map, waiting for God to speak to my spirit. After staring at the map for about fifteen minutes, I glanced at my watch and realized that it was time to brief my officers regarding their assignments. I quickly got up from my desk and went out into the squad room, where my officers were waiting for me to start the briefing.

I realized I had left my folder on my desk with information I wanted to pass on to my officers at the briefing. I returned to my office and again looked up at the carjacking offense map; I had not selected a deployment location for the task force. While looking at the map, my spirit directed my attention to W. 7 Mile Road and Southfield.

I didn't know why my spirit was directing me to W. 7 Mile and Southfield, because that area did not stand out differently than any of the other areas on West or East 7 Mile. What did stand out was that 7 Mile Road, East or West, was the worst location for carjackings in the city of Detroit.

I obeyed what my spirit was telling me and decided to deploy the Carjacking Task Force on West 7 Mile Road between Southfield and Outer Drive. I returned back to the squad room and informed the task force where they would be deployed on West 7 Mile Road. The officers gathered their equipment and proceeded to their assigned areas.

I remained at the office to prepare my personal map as to where each officer was deployed. Deployment means a specific assigned area or fixed location where an undercover officer is working in an unmarked, undercover surveillance vehicle. I keep track of where each officer is working and make notations on my personal map.

The type of fixed locations the Carjacking Task Force officers survey are businesses and locations where carjackings regularly occur. These locations are selected based upon crime data reported in carjackings. These locations usually are banks, gas stations, party stores, supermarkets, nightclubs, and drugstores, just to name a few.

After updating my personal map, I left the office and started heading towards the West 7 Mile Road and Southfield area. After arriving in the area, I started patrolling down West 7 Mile Road, looking at the businesses that would be the most likely target for carjackers. I arrived at West 7 Mile Road around 9:30 p.m.; activity on the road was getting busy. It was Friday night in July in Detroit, and I knew that the traffic would get much heavier because the partygoers had not come out yet.

After patrolling for a couple hours, I noticed heavy pedestrian and vehicular traffic near a gas station. Across the street from the gas station, there was also heavy pedestrian and vehicle traffic. I positioned my undercover police vehicle and parked in a parking lot adjacent to the party store and gas station. I sat in my car for about an hour, observing all the people coming in and out the gas station and party store.

I watched in amazement how careless people were going in and out of the gas station and party store. They were totally unconcerned or aware what was going around them. There were people standing and hanging around the gas station and party store. Some were approaching people asking for money from the customers. The customers let them walk right upon them without any concern that they may be robbed or carjacked. There were a lot of potential carjacking victims at this location.

Doing surveillance can sometimes be very boring, especially on weekdays. However, working on weekends, especially Friday and Saturday nights, can be exhilarating. You start to people watch, looking at the type and styles of clothing they were wearing. You have to closely monitor both your radios.

When conducting surveillance, you must monitor your surveillance car to car radio and monitor the precinct channel you are working in. This must be done so that undercover surveillance officers can monitor the activities of the uniformed officers in marked police vehicles. They need to be able to contact the dispatcher so their cover isn't blown or exposed.

Around 1 a.m., I heard a radio run come out on the precinct channel, that a woman was just robbed and carjacked at a party store on 7 Mile, east of Evergreen. The dispatcher gave out a description of the car and the license plate number. The dispatcher sent a marked unit to the location. I got on our surveillance radio and directed one of my surveillance units to the location, to interview the woman and get as much information as he could, and report back to me via cell phone. Seconds later, over the precinct channel, I heard another one of my surveillance officers announced that he was following the carjacked vehicle eastbound on West 7 Mile Road, occupied by four black males. My surveillance officer immediately asked the dispatcher to send a marked scout car to attempt to stop the driver in the carjacked vehicle. That night, the Carjacking Task Force was working in the 12th Precinct, one of the largest and busiest precincts in the city, and there were no available marked scout cars at that time.

My surveillance officer announced over the precinct channel that the carjacked vehicle had turned south on the Southfield Freeway service drive and drove onto the southbound Southfield Freeway. My surveillance officer continued following the vehicle and announced over the radio that the carjacked vehicle exited the freeway at the Grand River exit and was going southbound on the service drive towards South Rosedale Park, a prominent Detroit neighborhood. My officer announced that a marked unit from the 8th Precinct was now in charge of the pursuit. During this time, all twenty of my surveillance units had converged into the South Rosedale Park neighborhood and were monitoring the pursuit. The marked scout announced they had forced the carjacked vehicle into South Rosedale Park and that the vehicle was going westbound. Carjacking Task Forces officers had all the streets blocked going southbound, and the mark scout car announced that the vehicle had turned right onto Glastonbury Street. The rest of my surveillance units had the northbound streets blocked also. We had the carjacked vehicle trapped. The marked scout car unit announced that four suspects bailed out of the car and were running north. One of my surveillance units was on Glastonbury Street and observed all four suspects run into a house on the west side of Glastonbury Street. My officers exited their vehicles and covered the front door and back door of the residence.

I advised my officers not to go into the house until I got to the location. By this time, my surveillance unit that responded and interviewed the female victim on West 7 Mile Road, announced over our surveillance channel that the suspects were armed with a sawed-off shotgun, and that one of the suspects took her Louis Vuitton purse. I had all my surveillance officers rendezvous with me north of the address.

We discussed strategy on how we would enter the house the suspects ran into. I then contacted my officer at our office to start typing a search warrant and to get it signed as soon as possible. I knew we had a right to enter the house because we were in hot pursuit of the suspects, and my officers observed the fleeing suspects enter the house. I did not want to leave anything to chance that would interfere with convicting these dangerous suspects.

At this time, I decided I did not want to wait for the search warrant. I advised one of my surveillance officers to give me a blank consent-to-search form. I knew I was standing on solid legal ground if I searched the house and vehicle without a warrant. I called one of the uniform officers over to and advised him that I was going to knock on the door to see if someone would come and open it. I advised the officer to be extremely careful approaching the front door and said I would be in front of him. I explained that I needed him as a police presence, to ensure the person who opens the door knows we were the police. I got on the radio and advised the other officers at the scene what my intentions were. Things were pretty intense because we knew there were armed suspects inside the house.

The uniformed officer and I went up to the house, and I knocked on the door, announcing that we were the police. A man who appeared to be in his sixties opened the door. I advised the man that there were twenty-five police officers outside his house. I asked the man if he was owner of the home, and he stated that he was. I asked if he had a mortgage statement readily available that was in his name, and I asked him if I could see it. He stated I could see it and brought it back to the front door. I asked if he was aware of the young men who just entered his house, and he stated that he knew them. I advised him that they robbed and carjacked a woman and that they were armed with weapons, and I needed to get them out of the house safely, without anyone getting hurt. I advised the man that he needed to get everybody into the front living room and have everybody sit on the couch with both hands in the air.

I told him to explain that there were twenty-five officers on the scene and that there was nowhere to go. He stated that he would comply. I told him once he got everybody in the front living room, come back to front door and let me know. The man returned to his front door and advised me that everybody he was aware of was sitting in the front room with their hands up. I motioned to several of my surveillance officers to come onto the porch of the house, and I briefed them as to what was going on. We entered the house and observed five teenage males sitting on the couch with their hands in the air. I advised five of my surveillance officers and two of the uniform officers to handcuff the five young men sitting on the couch. I sent four of my surveillance officers to check upstairs and five of my officers to check the basement. After checking the upstairs, my officers found two more young men hiding in the attic.

After going down into the basement, two of my officers came back up and said to me, "We hit the jackpot; you need to come down and see this."

I went to the basement and saw numerous weapons laying out

on three long tables. I observed several automatic rifles including AK 47s and AR-10s; several handguns including Glocks, 9MM, .45 automatics; and an assortment of designer handbags, including Gucci, Louis Vuitton, Chanel, Donna Karan, and Coach. We found the badges of two police officers who were carjacked, and a reserve officer badge. We found a bag of jewelry consisting of assorted rings, watches, necklaces, gold chains, and wrist and ankle bracelets. We also found numerous wallets, male and female wallets. We also found small amounts of drugs and money.

We also found a leather pouch with eighteen sets of car keys belonging to assorted vehicles. I had one of my surveillance officers bring me the leather pouch. I poured the pouch of keys onto a table. I separated the keys into two sets of nine. I divided my surveillance officers into two teams of six officers. I advised them to check two blocks east, two blocks west, one block north, and one block south for the vehicles. Lo and behold, we hit the jackpot again. We were able to recover all eighteen vehicles, including several luxury vehicles: Cadillac Escalades, Lincoln Navigators, Mercedes Benzes, Jaguars, and BMWs.

After we processed all the evidence in the house and impounded all the vehicles, the Carjacking Task Force returned to the office to interview the suspects, conduct lineups, type warrants, and prepare reports. We were able to obtain confessions from six of the seven teenagers taken into custody. We positively tied them to forty-two carjackings and another possible twenty-eight carjackings. This was, and still is, the largest carjacking case solved in the history of Detroit. Because of the magnitude of the case, we decided to charge these suspects under the Federal RICO Statute in federal court. I contacted the chief on Saturday morning as directed. I updated him on the case, advising him of the number of arrests, number of cases closed, number of confessions, number of vehicles recovered, and number of weapons recovered.

Needless to say, the chief was ecstatic. He ended his conservation with me by saying, "Commander Napoleon, you did a great job."

We both laughed and hung up the phone. Two days earlier, before the case was solved, I was jokingly demoted two ranks, but now that the case has been solved, the chief jokingly promotes me upward two ranks. But, at the end of the day, I was still a lieutenant, my true rank.

People who don't believe there is a God would say that it was luck that helped me catch these carjacking perpetrators. Arrogant, ego-driven, self-centered police officers would say it was good instincts and good police work that led to this success. But when you compare luck and instinct to God, prayer, Holy Spirit, and discernment, you will find that God, prayer, and the Holy Spirit have a much greater record of success in a Christian's life than luck and instinct.

Luck and instinct are random and happen by chance, meaning it might happen and is not definitive. There are no other contributing factors that work in conjunction with luck or instinct.

Additionally, there is no avenue of communication with instinct or luck in which a person can confer with and have consistent success. As for God and prayer, the Holy Spirit is the definitive moving factor that leads a person to divine spiritual guidance, which leads a person to act and receive a positive outcome. Prayer provides the avenue for believers to communicate with God and ask for his guidance.

The success I had with solving the five cases mentioned earlier in this chapter had one main common denominator: prayer. Prayer provided the channel in which I could humbly communicate with God. This channel of communication allowed God to send his divine spirit, discernment, and guidance through the Holy Spirit within me, which led me to act in a way that led to success in all five cases. Prayer was the main common denominator; however, there were other factors that contributed to a positive outcome and success in all five cases. God as well as divine spiritual guidance, discernment, and the Holy Spirit were positive contributing factors.

One important thing that believers and nonbelievers in God must clearly understand: Even though you may go to God in prayer sincerely and humbly, there are times he will not answer those prayers. He will not answer a prayer that interferes with his will and his divine plans. God's will must be done over the will of man. Even though your request may seem simple and doable, it may interfere with God's will. People cannot see what's in the future, but the Lord can. Therefore, you should not lose faith in God if he does not answer all your prayers. However, if you live your life according to his mandates, he will answer your prayers many times more than he will reject them.

Many police officers claim to be Christians. However, their actions speak otherwise. Many of the people who stormed the US Capitol building claimed to be Christians. Many were active or retired police officers. Divine guidance was missing in their spirit, because they did not humbly go to God in prayer to seek his guidance and direction. The Holy Spirit is a restraining and controlling spirit.

If the people who stormed the Capitol did not give way to the evilness in their hearts, they would not have committed treason and attempt to overthrow democracy, which they claim to respect.

Policing in America is at a crossroad. The unnecessary violence and use of force perpetrated by police officers must end. America is a melting pot of diverse racial and ethnic citizens, and minorities must receive the same respect and equal treatment as whites. Thousands of hours of racial diversity training have done nothing to influence the attitudes and actions of racist police officers who are littered across American police departments. The real problem with racist police officers is they are devoid of any divine spiritual guidance and devoid of the positive controlling influence of God's Holy Spirit. They have nothing to help control their racism, hatred, and bigotry when interacting with blacks and other minorities. With the help of technology, their disgusting behavior has been revealed, and their lies have been exposed.

What I would truly like to see happen is a comprehensive study on those police officers who have committed heinous acts of violence against blacks and other minorities. I would be curious to know the answers to these questions:

1. What religious affiliation do they belong to or identify with?
2. How often do they attend church services during the year?
3. How often do they pray weekly?
4. How often do they read God's holy word, the Bible?
5. How often do they attend Bible study?
6. Have they ever been baptized?
7. How often do they take holy communion?
8. Do they accept Jesus as their Lord and Savior?

I would like to put these questions to all white police officers who were involved with shooting or killing unarmed minorities and those who used improper force. I believe we would discover that all their answers were consistent with each other.

I truly believe if you compared police officers who believe in God and Jesus, who attend church regularly, read the Bible and pray regularly, attend Bible study, are baptized, and accepted Jesus as their Lord and, Savior, you will find fewer incidents involving police shootings, excessive use of force, complaints of force, and citizen complaints. The reason for this difference is that officers who are believers have divine spiritual guidance and the controlling influence of God's Holy Spirit at their disposal. When sought after, believing officers make the right decisions and choices, because they are protected by the restraining influence of the Holy Spirit. The Holy Spirit is an ever-present spirit within those police officers who are believers in God and Jesus.

Unfortunately, unbelieving police officers depend on their own decision-making ability, which many times results in negative outcomes. Proverbs 14:12 states, "There is a way that seems right to a man, but in the end, it leads to death."

This scripture cannot be more true, applicable, and glaring pertaining to the actions of Officer Derek Chauvin murdering

George Floyd. Officer Chauvin truly believes in his own mind that his use of force was proper and right. He believes that choking a man for nine minutes and twenty-nine seconds was proper. Normal people would reason, how can an officer of the law think this way? However, unbelieving police officers do not have any protections against the god of this world, Satan, the devil. Unbelieving officers who are abusive to blacks and other minorities, and who use unjustified force, are being blinded by Satan, the devil.

This is clearly illustrated in 2 Corinthians 4:4, which states, "Satan, who is the god of this world, has blinded the minds of those who don't believe. They are unable to see the glorious light of the Good News. They don't understand this message about the glory of Christ, who is the exact likeness of God."

2 Corinthians 4:4 applies not only to police officers but to all unbelievers who refuse to accept and see the glorious light of the Good News. Unbelievers fail to realize that the purpose of Satan is to destroy this world and the people who reside in it. Satan's purpose is to keep the entire world in a state of unbelief in God and his Son Jesus. This is clearly delineated in John 8:44, which states, "For you are the children of your father the devil, and you love to do the evil things he does. He was a murderer from the beginning. He has always hated the truth, because there is no truth in him. When he lies, it is consistent with his character; for he is a liar and the father of lies." If unbelieving police officers continue to remain unprotected from Satan, the unjustified shooting of blacks and minorities will continue to escalate.

It is easy to sit back and criticize police officers when they are abusive to blacks and minorities. However, if the problems of racism and hatred are not properly discussed, America will wallow in its hatred, racism, discrimination, bigotry, and abuse.

As a believer in God and Jesus, I will direct my fellow officers to Bible scriptures that will greatly aid them and allow them to perform their duties that will be pleasing to God the Creator. If followed, many of the burdens police officers experience on a daily basis will be greatly eased. The following Bible verses will be helpful if followed:

"Trust in the LORD with all your heart; and lean not to your own understanding. In all your ways acknowledge him, and he will direct your path" (Proverbs 3:5–6). This is one of the most important and relevant Bible verses police officers can have at their disposal. Officers should place their trust and faith in God the Creator to direct them during the course of each day. Having this confidence that God is directing their path allows officers to be confident in the decisions they make.

"For GOD has not given us a spirit of fear, but of power and of love and of a sound mind" (2 Timothy 1:7). There have been many times where police officers have stated that they were in fear when they used force. In many cases, the suspect had no weapon, and officers still used excessive force. Police officers cannot do their jobs properly if they are in a constant state of fear. As this scripture says, God has given them the power to overcome fear. Because of this power given by the Lord, police officers should not attempt to perform their duties while in fear. God will be with you to overcome your fears.

"Create in me a clean heart, O God; and renew a right spirit within me" (Psalm 51:10). Police officers who have a difficult time dealing with racism, hatred, and bigotry need to know this scripture to clean up their heart. If police officers would humble themselves before God, this scripture is the first step toward healing, cleaning their hearts, and renewing a rightful spirit within. Having a right spirit will be extremely helpful when dealing with an impatient public. If sincere, this scripture is much more effective than any diversity training.

"Do not be quickly provoked in your spirit, for anger resides in the lap of fools" (Ecclesiastes 7:9). Too many times, police officers allow their ego, power, or insecurity to get in the way; this allows them to fall prey to their anger. This anger can escalate a situation and cause unnecessary conflict and grief. In times of conflict, a less volatile spirit will go a long way towards resolving the issue at hand.

"The LORD loves righteousness and justice; the earth is full of his unfailing love" (Psalm 33:5). God has encompassed the earth with his unfailing love. He commands us to love everyone, including our enemies. Love is the strongest force on the earth. If all police officers would follow and embrace love, it will greatly resonate with the ones we are called to protect and serve.

"He that follow after righteousness and mercy find life, righteousness, and honor" (Proverbs 21:21). Police officers must be righteous when enforcing the law. It is imperative that they dispense mercy equally and are fair to all they serve. Being righteous and showing mercy brings honor to those police officers who submit to the mandates of God's holy words.

"Love is patient, love is kind. It does not envy, it does not boast, it is not proud" (1 Corinthians 13:4). Police officers experience a multitude of different emotions while performing their duties. If love is put first above all things, it will make your immediate environment much more pleasant and beneficial to all. It will relieve tensions and allow for a more peaceful outcome.

Divine spiritual guidance is lacking in today's police environment. Trying to fight the forces of evil without divine guidance from God is putting police departments and police officers at a significant disadvantage and in jeopardy. The Lord wants his peacemakers to police with love, honor, righteousness, and truth. God wants his peacemakers to police with soundness of mind, spirit, and mercy, and not be quickly provoked or angered. I realize you cannot force or coerce police officers to utilize God's divine spiritual guidance. However, those police officers who believe in God and accept his Son Jesus as Lord and Savior use God's guidance daily in discharging their duties. They are experiencing daily the truth and promises of God's holy word while discharging their duties as police officers.

9

OBSTACLES TO POLICE REFORM

They will fight against you, but they will not overcome you, for I am with you to deliver you. (Jeremiah 1:19)

IN TODAY'S SOCIETY, THERE IS a vociferous call for police reform because of unjustified, excessive, and fatal use of force against black people and other minorities. This excessive use of force occurs much too often, and many instances, the police officers are not being held accountable for their actions. Even when this brutality and fatal force have been captured on camera, prosecution of the offending officers has been limited or nonexistent.

Across the country, political and religious leaders, concerned citizens, and activists are being mobilized to find solutions to this devasting problem. Remedies such as diversity and racial sensitivity training, law enforcement policy changes, and police reform have been proposed as solutions to the unjust incidents of police brutality and the use of fatal force.

However, leaders are focused on finding solutions without examining the underlying causes of excessive force against black people and other minorities. There are clear-cut causes that drive excessive force by police officers, but these causes are not being aggressively addressed.

Nationwide, a major obstacle driving the improper use of force by police officers is police unions. Now, I want to make it perfectly clear that I am not anti-union. I was a member of the UAW while employed by General Motors and a member of the police union my entire career while serving in the Detroit Police Department. Unions are necessary to negotiate fair wages for their membership and to protect their members from tyrannical and abusive police supervision and leadership. However, the problem is that unions often overstep their boundaries and attempt to control a police department.

Police unions are very active in the political process. Many unions have political action committees, and depending on the size of the membership, they have significant monetary resources to contribute to candidates who support law enforcement concerns. This support includes financial donations to the campaigns of prosecutors, governors, mayors, city council members, state legislators, senators, congressional representatives, and presidential candidates. These donations give police unions massive power, support, and influence. The unions use this influence against progressive, reformed-minded police chiefs. The unions' power and influence are sometimes detrimental to the operation of the police department and detrimental to the community and citizens the department serves.

One of the most significant detriments nationwide is when police unions blindly support and defend an officer's actions, regardless of the seriousness of the violation the officer has committed. This unbridled support becomes problematic when officers commit violations against citizens they are charged with the duty to protect and serve. This blind support by police unions destroys the police department's image, eliminates law enforcement's integrity, negatively affects community relations, and erodes community confidence in the department.

Another significant obstacle to police reform is binding arbitration in a department's disciplinary proceedings. Arbitrators should not be the final decision-makers in police disciplinary cases. All too often, arbitrators have sided with police unions when severe violations occur. Arbitrators are civilians, and in many cases, they have judged police officers as though they are civilians, and rendered judgments in their favor from a civilian perspective. For instance, if someone who works in the auto industry gets drunk off duty, he won't receive discipline from his employer because he is off-duty. However, police officers are obliged to carry their weapons at all times. Therefore, if officers get drunk, they must be disciplined. Arbitrators have historically and consistently given officers a free pass in such cases.

Arbitrators have also failed to terminate police officers with abundant disciplinary histories. This includes restoring the employment of officers with histories of excessive force and other serious violations of police department rules and regulations. Without court intervention, police unions will never surrender arbitration, even if arbitration decisions are detrimental to the police department and the community.

Another obstacle to police reform is the gender and racial composition of police union leadership—typically white and male nationwide. This lack of diversity is detrimental because only one view is represented in decision-making, in community relations, in endorsements and donations to political candidates, and in the functions and governance of the union.

Union officials are not concerned about diversity in a department's upper management or promotions. Nor are they concerned about affirmative action, racial equality, and police reform. The attitudes of some white officers regarding equal rights for black people were reflected in a survey conducted in 2017. According to the Pew Research Center, which surveyed eight thousand police officers nationwide, 92 percent of white officers believe the United States has already achieved equal rights for black people, while only 29 percent of black officers do. And while only 27 percent of white officers believe that protests against police violence are motivated at least in part by a genuine desire for accountability, roughly 70 percent of black officers held that view.

Police unions have historically challenged affirmative action in hiring and promotion practices. In the mid-1970s, the Detroit Police Officers Association and Detroit Police Lieutenants and Sergeants Association unions, which were controlled by white police officers, fought against reform and affirmative action for hiring and promotions in the Detroit Police Department.

At that time, the Detroit Police Department had a force of five thousand police officers, 97 percent of whom were white. The population of the city was 55 percent black and 45 percent white. The Detroit Police Department was viewed as an occupying army because of its abuse of force against black people. In 1974, the Board of Police Commissioners of the City of Detroit adopted a voluntary affirmative action plan to remedy what it perceived as a history of discriminatory practices in the hiring and promotion of blacks in the Detroit Police Department. The Board set as its goal a fifty-fifty ratio of blacks to whites for staffing in all levels. Under Detroit's affirmative action plan, two promotion lists were established, one for black officers and one for white officers. Promotions were made alternately from one list and then the other, thereby guaranteeing that fifty percent of subsequent promotees would be black. The Detroit Police Officers Union and Detroit Police Lieutenants and Sergeants Union fought against reform and affirmative action. It was determined in court proceedings that the Detroit Police Department had a documented history of racial discrimination and bias against black officers and black applicants in its hiring and promotion practices. Both police unions spent tens of thousands of union dollars to fight against the interests of black police officers who were members of these unions and who had paid union dues while they served the city. When it comes to equality issues and diversity, unions that are predominantly white do not care about the interest of black officers who are members of their union. This was clearly delineated in the article entitled "Crackdown Detroit: Affirmative Action in the Detroit Police Department," a project of the Policing and Social Justice History Lab, an initiative of the University of Michigan Department of History and U-M Carceral State Project:

> In 1973, Black Detroiters cries for police reform and integration won a major victory through the election of Coleman Young. Young was the first African American Mayor in Detroit's history and he ran on a platform largely centered around police reform. After his election, Coleman Young made immediate efforts to help bring more African-Americans into the police force. He did so largely through an affirmative action program which sought to hire and promote more black officers within the Detroit Police Department. Additionally, Young tried to bring in and promote a greater number of female officers. Over the course of his administration, Young's police department continued to use affirmative action policies to help improve the representation of African Americans and women within the police department.
>
> On July 31, 1974, the Board of Police Commissioners adopted a resolution ordering the police chief to implement affirmative action in the hiring and promotion of minorities, and to take

further steps to eliminate discrimination in the pre-existing criteria for hiring and promotions. By December of the following year, the police department had created a policy ensuring the promotion of an equal number of black and white officers. Under the new policy, black and white candidates above a certain benchmark score were ranked on two separate lists. Each time a candidate was selected for a promotion from the top of the white list, another candidate was also selected from the top of the black list. That system was eventually expanded to include white and black women in the order of promotions. White male officers and the largely white police union fought against these policies through lawsuits and protests From 1974 until the mid-80's the Detroit Police Officer's Union, despite their claims of representing both black and white officers, pursued every possible legal avenue to block the integration of the Detroit Police Department. By mid1975, both the Detroit Police Lieutenants and Sergeants Association and the Detroit Police Officers Association had filed lawsuits in the United States District Court in Detroit against Mayor Young, the Detroit Police Department, and the city of Detroit itself, alleging that the affirmative action program was unconstitutional and violated labor agreements. The United States District Court ruled in favor of the City of Detroit, and the unions appealed the decision to the United States Court of Appeals, Sixth Circuit, which ruled in favor of the City of Detroit on July 29, 1987.

By 1993 the Detroit Police Department managed to achieve an even split between white and black officers, finally succeeding in creating a police force that was more representative of Detroit's racial demographics.

Police unions exposed their racism, careless judgment, fragility, moral character, and lack of decency by supporting Donald Trump for president in 2016 and 2020. Every major police union in America supported Trump, despite Trump's documented racism, discriminatory actions against blacks and Hispanics in his attempt to deny renting to blacks and Hispanics. Police unions supported him in spite of numerous allegations of sexual assaults, marriage infidelity, his acknowledged grabbing and improperly touching women, misuse of his charity, his failure to pay contractors, his numerous bankruptcies, and his telling over two thousand documented lies while in office as president. Choosing to support a racist candidate and President makes political leaders and the black community wonder if unions are even interested in police reform or improving their police departments. Support of such a flawed candidate reflects on the judgment, decency, character, morality, and fairness of police unions. It questions and reflects on whether or not police union members can provide honest, fair, and equal law enforcement services to black and minority communities.

Yet another obstacle to police reform is police unions' planned attacks against reformed-minded police chiefs. Police unions will use every tactic in their nationwide universal playbook to get rid of police chiefs, especially police chiefs who were hired from outside of the police department and who hold union members accountable. Police chiefs hired outside the department usually only last about three or four years, if that long. They may last the four-year term of the mayors who hired them, but not much longer than that.

When police union members decide to activate their playbook, they usually have a set of actions they use to gain the support of the community and destroy the police chief's standing with the people who hired him or her.

These actions include (1) going behind the police chief's back and complaining to the mayor, city manager, and city council about the chief's leadership skills; (2) complaining that the chief micro-manages the department; (3) complaining that the chief is destroying the morale of the department; (4) complaining that the chief shows favoritism towards certain officers; (5) accusing the chief of regularly violating the union contract; (6) accusing the chief of bad decision-making; (7) accusing the chief of having different, uneven accountability standards for certain police officers; (8) accusing the chief of not providing police officers enough training; (9) making allegations about the chief to community leaders; (10) conducting a planned, organized, misguided, unjustified vote of no-confidence against the chief; (11) leaking false information to the news media. Police unions are relentless in their efforts to destroy the reputation of police chiefs they feel they can't control or manipulate.

There are certain things newly hired police chiefs should do in order to survive and to protect themselves against unjustified attacks and false allegations by police union leaders. These actions include (1) meeting individually with the mayor, city manager, and city council members as soon as possible. Advise them of your plans for the department, explain your leadership style, and let them know that officers will be coming to them to complain about you. Address any concerns they may have. (2) Meet with community leaders and listen to their concerns regarding any issues they have with the police department and police officers. (3) Meet with union leaders and listen to their concerns. (4) Meet with the command officers to address their concerns and communicate your expectations of them. (5) Meet with the media and request that they give you a chance to respond to any officer complaints prior to releasing media stories. These actions will go a long way in protecting police chiefs from unjust attacks from police unions and their members.

Another obstacle to police reform is politicians and the political structure they operate in. There is very little accountability for elected officials once elected. Accountability only comes into play during election time. Most ordinary citizens have short attention spans and do not keep track of the actions and decisions made by the people they elect.

Politicians give politically correct sound bites to the media during calls for police reform to pacify citizens, but nothing gets done, or police reform gets put on hold or gets neglected. Police reform cost money, and many politicians do not want to budget money for police reform, which could interfere with pet projects they believe would be more beneficial to their political future.

Most citizens would think that police union leaders would be open to reform in their department. Yes, leaders should represent their membership, but they should not protect their members when they cross the line and use abusive or unnecessary force against citizens.

Another significant obstacle to police reform is the shrinking tax base of many American cities. Shrinking city tax revenues have a profound effect on police budgets. Police budgets have been significantly reduced nationwide. Many police departments are struggling just to provide basic services. Calls for police accountability, use-of-force training, diversity training, technology improvements, bias training, and racial sensitivity training put a tremendous strain on cities to provide additional resources to expand and increase police budgets. It is nearly impossible for struggling cities to add revenue to their police department budgets.

In order for citizens to understand what obstacles confront police chiefs as they strive to lead their departments, I would like to provide you with some of my experiences while serving as chief of the Inkster, Michigan, Police Department.

Inkster is a small Michigan community of approximately twenty-five thousand residents, located approximately five miles from Detroit's western border. The racial makeup of the city is approximately 60 percent black and 40 percent white. Prior to the layoffs, the Inkster Police Department was 75 percent white officers and 25 percent black officers. Shortly after becoming chief, I was notified by the city manager that Inkster was experiencing severe revenue shortfalls. The city manager told me I had to reduce my $8 million budget to $2.5 million. The reason for the severe revenue shortfalls was that the state of Michigan cut Inkster's revenue sharing by $1.5 million; Inkster experienced a significant shortfall in the water budget, and the city experienced revenue shortfalls because of twenty-two hundred home foreclosures.

I advised the city manager that it would take significant reductions in police operations to reach that figure, and he advised me that if the city did not balance the budget, the state of Michigan would appoint an emergency manager; city department heads would not have any decision-making authority regarding their budget nor have any decision-making authority to run their department. The city manager said that we could not let that happen and we had to make the necessary cuts in all city departments.

The city manager advised me to prepare a report with the necessary requirements to meet the requested reductions. I met with all of the police unions and advised them what had to be done. I asked the police unions what would be the maximum pay reduction their members would take to prevent layoffs. All of the union leaders stated their members would not take any reductions in pay. I advised them of the consequences if no reductions were taken, but they all stood by their decisions of no reductions in pay.

As chief of police, I had to weigh public safety with the city's ability to provide sufficient revenue for police services. I prepared three different budget scenarios that would get the police budget to $2.5 million. The first budget scenario I prepared dealt with saving as many police positions as possible. The only way this could be done is if the unions would agree to take significant pay reductions of 25 percent. I knew the unions would not agree, but I had to try for the sake of the citizens and public safety. The second budget scenario I prepared dealt with no pay cuts but would significantly deplete police department personnel. The third budget scenario had a 10 percent pay reduction and fewer officer layoffs.

I again met with the police unions and presented the three budget reduction scenarios I had prepared. I gave them time to review each scenario and determine the scenario that would be most acceptable. Union representatives advised me that none of the scenarios were acceptable. I advised the unions that if we did not make the necessary cuts, the state of Michigan would take over the city budget and make the cuts necessary to balance the city budget. I advised the union representatives of the details of the city's revenue shortfalls. The union representatives advised me that the city needed to find the money to fund the police department, and the unions would not agree to any reductions in pay or other police benefits. I advised the union representatives that the city had no funds to maintain the police department at its current staffing level and explained that there would be significant police layoffs.

Because of the revenue shortfalls, I had to lay off 75 percent of police department personnel, including the janitor, animal control officer, records clerk, and secretary. I went from eighty-three police personnel down to twenty-five officers, including myself. Needless to say, you will not be able to do any type of training with such a sizeable reduction in police personnel. Reduced state revenue sharing, and shrinking city revenues present a significant obstacle to providing the necessary training for police reform. Additional training is costly, and if revenues are not available, the training cannot be done.

Inkster is not the only city experiencing budget issues and issues with funding for police departments. I spoke to other police chiefs in the county at our quarterly meetings; approximately twenty-eight of the forty-two police departments in the county were experiencing some kind of budget and funding issues. The police chief in a city adjacent to Inkster was working as that city's police chief and city manager. Four cities merged their fire departments to reduce costs and save money. Clearly, the lack of sufficient revenues for cities is an obstacle to police reform, because police departments will not have the money needed to provide the necessary training and technology to reform police departments across America. City revenues affect police budgets, technology, and training.

Technology plays a significant role in providing obstacles to police reform. How? Many businesses use technology to eliminate tax-paying workers and replace them with machines. Human workers pay taxes, not machines. Taxes paid by humans fund police departments nationwide. Corporate greed and technology have played a significant role in reducing tax revenues for cities that were once paid by working human beings. People are being replaced with self-check-out machines at supermarket chains, hardware stores, drugstores, banks, car washes, and gas stations; there are self-driving delivery vehicles all across the country. Cities are suffering significant losses in tax revenues because of the replacement of human beings by technology. This causes revenues shortages that could be used to reform police departments.

10

REAL SOLUTIONS

Many are the afflictions of the righteous, but the Lord delivers him out of them all. (Psalm 34:19)

AMERICA IS IN TURMOIL BECAUSE of bad decisions by police officers regarding the unjustified use of force and the shooting of unarmed black citizens and other minorities. These incidents have resulted in millions of dollars in lawsuits, as well as millions of dollars to business owners as a result of businesses being damaged or destroyed by rioting. These incidents of unjustified use of force and shooting of black and minority citizens is occurring much too frequently across America. Too often, officers involved in these unjustified shootings have not been disciplined or prosecuted; usually, their police chiefs do not hold them accountable.

Jesus clearly states in Mark 3:24, "If a kingdom be divided against itself, that kingdom cannot stand." There cannot be two separate justice systems in America. The country will not survive if it continues to do nothing about injustice to black citizens. Today, the kingdom of America is severely divided, and unless it lives up to its creed, that all men and women are created equal, it will fall to its discrimination, racism, anger, hatred, bigotry, and greed.

As a law enforcement executive, I worked in three different police departments, the Detroit Police Department being the largest. I have worked in a variety of diversified assignments, such as Gang Enforcement, Homicide (as a detective sergeant), and the Carjacking Task Force, just to name a few. I am a graduate of the FBI National Academy and possess a master's degree. I served as chief of police in Inkster and in Highland Park. The Detroit Police Department during my career was 55 percent black and 45 percent white. The Inkster and Highland Park Police Departments were both 75 percent white and 25 percent black. I believe that my thirty-three years in law enforcement gives me the perspective to suggest what needs to be done to correct the problems regarding unjustified use of force and police shootings. Some of these recommendations may be considered extreme and controversial, but they will deter the improper use of force and eliminate unjustified shootings of unarmed citizens by police officers.

I believe the following policies should be considered:

National Standard Policy for Use of Force

This policy should be developed by a racially diversified panel of police chiefs and police executives. When selecting this panel, consideration should be given to experience, size of department, race, gender, training, and education. Priority focus should be given to police shootings of unarmed suspects. The panel should write a policy that eliminates all historical police catchphrases used in the past to justify improper use of force. Reports involving police shootings and use of force nationwide should be utilized to identify these phrases. These catchphrases include "I was in fear for my life. He made a furtive gesture. I thought he was armed. He rushed at me. I saw [or he had] a shiny object" and any other phrase used to validate an unjust shooting. Priority focus should also be given to what constitutes a life-threatening weapon, other than guns and knives. Fingernail clippers, car keys, pop and beer cans, jump ropes, and garbage can lids should not be considered lethal weapons. Police officers are aware of the dangers of police work when they choose to serve. They are equipped with bulletproof vests. Therefore, police officers must take the greater risk when confronting citizens and must be certain that a suspect is armed with a gun or life-threatening weapon. "I thought he had," "it looked like he had," "I was in fear," "he reached in his pocket," "he had a shiny object," and other historical phrases should no longer be accepted when a police officer shoots an unarmed person. Shooting unarmed citizens by police officers must stop.

National Standard Disciplinary Data Base for Police Officers

A national disciplinary data base should be developed for all police agencies nationwide. This data base should contain the disciplinary history of all police officers. This will prevent problem officers from concealing their disciplinary history and getting hired in another state. This data base should include all instances where police officers have resigned under charges, prior to their hearing or final disposition. This data base will greatly assist police departments in hiring good officers.

National Standard Policy for Less-Than-Lethal Force Alternative

A national policy should be developed for less-than-lethal force alternatives, such as pepper spray, batons, tasers, projectile launchers, beanbags, and other alternative sources. This policy must include training and instruction in the use of all approved less-than-lethal force alternatives. This policy should be read at police roll calls biweekly, as well as the use of force policy.

National Standard for Diversity in Hiring Practices and Promotions

It is imperative that police departments nationwide reflect the pluralistic makeup of the communities they serve in their hiring and promotion practices. There are too many police departments that are lacking in diversity and do not reflect the entire community they serve. The lack of diversity causes distrust in minority communities, who feel they are not being represented. When police departments embrace diversity in hiring and promotions, citizens feel they have representatives who are fair and can relate to the issues and problems in their communities. This diversity includes the hiring of female officers and other minorities reflected in a specific community. Police departments should assign minority officers to patrol minority neighborhoods as often as possible.

National Standard for Diversity Training

A national policy for diversity training should be developed for police departments nationwide. It is imperative that this training be conducted in police departments, to debunk the myths and stereotyping of black citizens and other minorities.

The stereotyping of minorities is the fuel that supports racism and distorts the thought process of police officers who buy into its false distortion of minorities. Some police officers buy into the stereotyping of black people, and it causes problem for them when interacting with them on a daily basis. All black men are not drug dealers and crackheads, and all black women are not welfare queens. This type of stereotyping by police officers contributes to the erosion of trust in the communities they serve.

National Standard Legislative Laws for Police Officers Shooting Unarmed Suspects and Use of Excessive Force

Being a police officer is one of the most difficult jobs in society. Police officers deal with murderers, rapists, robbers, and other criminals on a regular basis. However, it is imperative that police officers do not cross the line when using force in arresting suspects for minor violations. Using improper force decimates the trust citizens have in their police officers. It causes civil upheaval, riots, and unnecessary demonstrations. In this present-day environment where nearly every citizen has a cell phone with video capabilities, officers must be careful how they conduct themselves when utilizing force. Because of this technology, overly aggressive police officers nationwide have been exposed and their improper actions documented via cell phone video. Therefore, it is imperative that legislation be passed to ensure that police officers are held accountable for excessive force perpetrated in cases involving minor violations. Additionally, new laws must be passed to ensure mandatory prison sentences for police officers who shoot unarmed suspects or recklessly use unnecessary force. Holding police officers accountable is a major concern in minority communities, and major changes are necessary.

National Review Board for Prosecutors and Police Chiefs

Prosecutors are elected officials with close ties to police departments and police unions. Additionally, there are some police chiefs who believe they should protect their officers at all costs, which greatly compromises their integrity. In cases of fatal or excessive force, or shooting unarmed suspects, their actions should be reviewed by this national review board to ensure the actions were proper under the circumstances presented.

National Standard for Reviewing Police Officer and Scout Car Videos

There must be a national standard for reviewing police officer and scout car video footage on a regular basis. This must be done in order to promptly detect any improper use of force by police officers, so the incident can be investigated and witnesses to the incident identified. Some incidents of improper use of force were detected months or even years after the initial incident occurred. This delay prevents the collection of evidence to conduct a fair and impartial investigation. Delays brings into question the sincerity of police departments to get to the truth.

National Standards for Discharging Police Officers for Severe Policy Violations

On too many occasions, police officers were not disciplined or discharged because the prosecutor decided not to prosecute them. Serious police department violations have been swept under the carpet by police chiefs and no discipline given to the offending officers. National criteria must be developed to ensure that officers who are not prosecuted are discharged from departments when departmental policies are violated.

I developed these solutions as a result of my extensive experience in police work. These solutions will be debated and discussed amongst those who read this book. People may say my solutions are too hard on police officers and police departments. Other people will agree with my assessment. Only if implemented can we say for sure whether my solutions will be effective in reducing the number of shootings of unarmed citizens and the improper use of force.

However, I have other solutions that I would like to provide that some will say are just as controversial as the ones provided earlier in this chapter.

The best solutions to the problems in policing can be found in the Bible by the words of God almighty. I had formal training regarding the Bible and attended Bible college, but I am not a pastor or minister. I am a believer in God the Creator, and his Son Jesus Christ. I am obligated as a Christian to bring lost souls to Jesus and spread the good news of the Gospel. As a police officer and as police chief, I have personally seen God Almighty act on my behalf to help solve some crimes and guide my decision-making. I regularly prayed to God during my career to never allow me to shoot anyone or use fatal force upon anyone. During my thirty-three years in police work, God answered my prayers. I never shot anyone, and I was never accused of using excessive force or injuring a prisoner. I hope that people realize the realness of God's power to change things and situations.

Before I go into the solutions of God's word, I would like to provide you with an example of God's infinite power and guidance. While I was commanding officer of the Carjacking Task Force, we received a report of a carjacking of a prominent doctor in Indian Village, an upscale Detroit neighborhood. The suspects drove the doctor's car to a nearby suburb, where they forced their way into a woman's vehicle and raped her in front of her two-year-old daughter and eighteen-month-old son. I responded to the scene and was infuriated by what occurred. I returned to my office, closed the door, and prayed to God for help solving this heinous crime. We had no clues, no suspects, and no witnesses.

I enlisted all officers assigned to the Carjacking Task Force to solve this crime. We received information via police teletype that the car of the woman who was raped was recovered in Toledo, Ohio. We also received information that the suspects committed a home invasion and carjacking in Toledo. At this time, spiritual discernment came over me. The only clue we had was a description of the car taken in Toledo. Finding this car was like finding a needle in a haystack. My discernment led me to assign my task force officers to different downriver cities near the Interstate 75 corridor, hoping to identify the vehicle the suspects were driving.

Through the grace of God, one of my officers spotted the vehicle south of Detroit. My officer was following closely in an undercover surveillance vehicle. We frantically tried to contact the local authorities to request a marked police vehicle to stop the wanted suspects.

Before we were able to make contact, the suspects became suspicious and sped off at a high rate of speed. My surveillance officer attempted to keep up, but I had to cut the chase off because my officer was in an undercover unmarked vehicle, and I could not allow him to endanger the public because his vehicle had no lights or sirens.

The suspects conducted three more carjackings in nearby cities. Finally, we received information that the last car the suspects carjacked was found burned up in the projects in a city that bordered Detroit. We canvassed the area but could not find any witnesses because the burnt vehicle was discovered late at night. After spending hours in the area, I ordered the task force back to the office to prepare an after-action report of the incident. While sitting in my surveillance car updating my boss, I was approached by a young teenager who began to compliment me on the car. He said my car looked just like the car that was burned up on the railroad tracks.

I asked, "Why would somebody burn up such a nice car like that?"

He stated that the vehicle was probably stolen because he saw two dudes walking away from the car and pointed to the house they went into. A statement was taken from the young man as to what he had observed. I became overjoyed and started praising God internally.

The young man left the area, not knowing he helped solve one of the most heinous crimes a person can commit. I telephoned my office, advised one of my officers to type up a search warrant, and directed the rest of the task force officers back to my location to execute the search warrant. The judge signed the search warrant, and the task force executed the warrant and arrested both of the involved suspects. Confessions were taken from both suspects, and all concerned police departments were notified. The suspects were subsequently convicted of the rape and carjacking of the woman and sentenced to forty to sixty years in prison.

During the course of my lengthy and diversified career, I've seen the difference between great police work and divine intervention. It was divine intervention from God that solved this case. We searched hours for witnesses in the projects and found none. No evidence could be obtained from the car because it was totally destroyed by fire. But God sent that young man to me, who unknowingly provided the crucial information needed to solve this crime. Matthew 7:7 states, "Ask and it shall be given to you, seek and you shall find." When I prayed to God for guidance and asked for his assistance, he allowed me to find a person to help solve this crime. On many occasions, especially while working at Homicide and Carjacking, God answered my prayers and provided me with information that helped solve crimes.

Police chiefs, prosecutors, and police officers should consider the following scriptures when discharging their duties:

"Trust in the LORD with all your heart; and lean not to your own understanding. In all your ways acknowledge him, and he will direct your path" (Proverbs 3:5–6). This is one of the most important and relevant Bibles verses police officers can have at their disposal. Officers should place their trust and faith in God the Creator to direct them during the course of each day. Believing that God is directing their path allows officers to be confident in the decisions they make.

"Create in me a clean heart, O GOD, and renew within me a right spirit" (Psalm 51:10). Some police officers have a difficult time dealing with racism, hatred, and bigotry; this is the scripture they need to know to clean up their heart. If police officers humble themselves before God, this scripture will heal their hearts and renew their spirit. Having a right spirit will be extremely helpful when dealing with an impatient public. If sincere, this scripture is much more effective than any diversity training.

"In all things, do unto others as you would have them to do unto you" (Matthew 7:12). Police officers must be constantly mindful that they are obligated to treat all people the way they want to be treated. This treatment must filter down to people officers take into custody. Unequal treatment by law enforcement officers is the biggest issue facing police departments nationwide. If police officers would just follow God's word, it would make their job much easier on those occasions they must take someone into custody.

"For GOD has not given us a spirit of fear, but of power and of love and of a sound mind" (2 Timothy 1:7). Many times, police officers have stated they were in fear when they were involved in the use of force. In many cases, the suspect had no weapon, but officers still used excessive force. Police officers cannot do their jobs properly if they are in a constant state of fear. As this scripture says, God has given them the power to overcome fear. Because of this power, police officers should not attempt to perform their duties while in fear. God will help you overcome your fears.

"Judge me favorably, O LORD, because I have walked with integrity and I have trusted you without wavering" (Psalm 26:1). Law enforcement officers who fail to police with integrity and fairness, and abuse their trust, will not be judged favorably by the Lord. Those officers who walk in integrity, honesty, truthfulness, equality, and fairness will be favorably judged by God the Creator.

"Examine me, O LORD, and test me. Look closely into my heart and mind. I see your mercy in front of me. I walk in the light of your truth. I did not sit with liars, and I will not be found among hypocrites. I have hated the mob of evil doers, and will not sit with wicked people. I will wash my hand in innocence" (Psalm 26:2 -6). Police officers will be judged by what is in their hearts and minds, and not by any deceptive words or actions that they may display. God always judges by what's in a person's heart and mind; he is not deceived by insincere words or actions. Only the pure in heart shall see God.

"Have I not commanded you? Be strong and courageous. Do not be frightened, and do not be dismayed, for the Lord your God is with you wherever you go" (Joshua 1:9). A scared and frightened officer can be reckless and dangerous. Many times, officers use fear as an excuse to shoot someone unnecessarily. God did not give his believers the spirit of fear. He is with you wherever you go and will be a calming influence to assist you in making the right decisions in times of confrontation and chaos.

"Give justice to the weak and the fatherless; maintain the right of the afflicted and the destitute. Rescue the weak and the needy; deliver them from the hand of the wicked" (Psalm 82:3–4).

The scriptures provided in this chapter will greatly assist police chiefs, police officers, and prosecutors in discharging their duties on a daily basis, if taken with a humble spirit. I know there are many police officers who are not true believers in God or Jesus. Officers who are not grounded in the word of God are the ones who shoot unarmed citizens and use excessive force. These officers are discharging their duties without the protection of the Holy Spirit. Their minds and spirits are left unprotected and are subjected to the wiles of the devil, Satan. Satan's purpose is to steal, kill, and destroy humankind. Unprotected police officers succumb to Satan's deception, destroy their careers, and severely damage the image of police departments nationwide.

2 Corinthians 4:4 states, "Satan, who is the god of this world, has blinded the minds of those who don't believe. They are unable to see the glorious light of the Good News. They don't understand this message about the glory of Christ, who is the exact likeness of God." God does not want his peacemakers to police in fear and blindness, or be subjected to the deception of the devil. God wants his peacemakers to be strong and courageous; they should police with clean hearts, right spirits, and integrity. He wants his peacemakers to police with love, honor, righteousness, and truth. God wants his peacemakers to police with soundness of mind, spirit, and mercy, and not be quickly provoked or angered. He has provided his peacemakers with the necessary armor to protect themselves while discharging their official duties. God's peacemakers should familiarize themselves with the following Bible verses to stand firm and resist the evil of Satan.

Ephesians 6:10–17 states, "Finally, be strong in the Lord and in the strength of His might. Put on the full armor of God, so that you will be able to stand firm against the schemes of the devil. For our struggle is not against flesh and blood, but against the rulers, against the powers, against the world forces of this darkness, against the spiritual forces of wickedness in the heavenly places. Therefore, take up the full armor of God, so that you will be able to resist on the evil day, and having done everything, to stand firm. Stand firm therefore, having belted your waist with truth, and having put on the breastplate of righteousness, and having strapped on your feet the preparation of the gospel of peace; in addition to all, taking up the shield of faith with which you will be able to extinguish all the flaming arrows of the evil one. And take the helmet of salvation and the sword of the Spirit, which is the word of God."

May the love, grace, mercy, and peace of GOD the Creator abide with all my brothers and sisters in law enforcement. May this book be a blessing to all who read it.